Sit & Solve™

HARD SUDOKU

Michael Rios

Sterling Publishing Co., Inc.
New York

4 6 8 10 9 7 5

Published by Sterling Publishing Co., Inc.
387 Park Avenue South, New York, NY 10016
© 2005 by Michael Rios
Distributed in Canada by Sterling Publishing
c/o Canadian Manda Group, 165 Dufferin Street,
Toronto, Ontario, Canada M6K 3H6
Distributed in the United Kingdom by GMC Distribution Services,
Castle Place, 166 High Street, Lewes, East Sussex, England BN7 1XU
Distributed in Australia by Capricorn Link (Australia) Pty. Ltd.
P.O. Box 704, Windsor, NSW 2756, Australia

Sit & Solve is a trademark of Sterling Publishing Co., Inc.

Sterling ISBN-13: 978-1-4027-3593-6
ISBN-10: 1-4027-3593-6

For information about custom editions, special sales, premium and
corporate purchases, please contact Sterling Special Sales
Department at 800-805-5489 or specialsales@sterlingpub.com.

CONTENTS

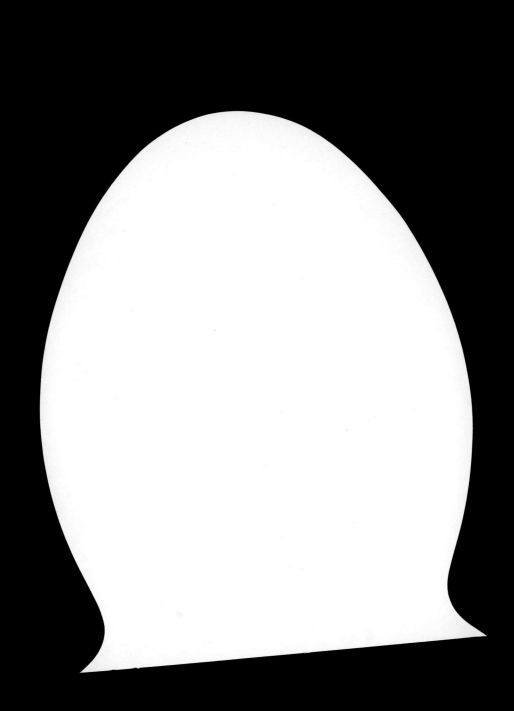

To solve sudoku puzzles, all you need to know is this one simple rule:

Fill in the boxes so that each of the nine rows, each of the nine columns, and each of the nine 3x3 sections contain all the numbers from 1 to 9.

And that's all there is to it! Using these simple rules, let's see how far we get on this sample puzzle at right. (The letters at the top and left edges of the puzzle are for reference only; you won't see them in the regular puzzles.)

The first number that can be filled in is an obvious one: box EN is the only blank box in the center 3x3 section, and all the digits 1 through 9 are represented except for 5. EN must be 5.

The next box is a little trickier to dis-cover. Consider the upper left 3x3 section of the puzzle. Where can a 4 go? It can't go in AK, BK, or CK because row K

	A	B	C	D	E	F	G	H	I
J									
K				2		1	8	4	
L	9		5	7		2	6		
M	1	4	3	9	2		7		
N		7		6					
O	7		1	4	8	9		2	
P	3	2		6		8		5	
Q	8	4	9	3					
R									

5

already has a 4 at IK. It can't go in BJ or BL because column B already has a 4 at BQ. It can't go in CJ because column C already has a 4 at CM. So it must go in AJ.

Another box in that same section that can now be filled is BJ. A 2 can't go in AK, BK, or CK due to the 2 at EK. The 2 at GL rules out a 2 at BL. And the 2 at CP means that a 2 can't go in CJ. So BJ must contain the 2. It is worth noting that this 2 couldn't have been placed without the 4 at AJ in place. Many of the puzzles rely on this type of steppingstone behavior.

We now have a grid as shown. Let's examine column A. There are four blank boxes in column A; in which blank box must the 2 be placed? It can't be AK because of the 2 in EK (and the 2 in BJ). It can't be AO because of the 2 in IO. It can't be AR because of the 2 in CP. Thus, it must be AN that has the 2.

	A	B	C	D	E	F	G	H	I
J	4	2			2		1	8	4
K	9			5		7		2	6
L			4	3	9	2			7
M	1			7	5	6			
N	7			1	4	8	9		2
O							6	8	5
P	3		2		6				
Q	8	4	9		3				
R									

By the 9's in AL, EM, and CQ, box BN must be 9. Do you see how?

We can now determine the value for box IM. Looking at row M and then column I, we find all the digits 1 through 9 are represented but 8. IM must be 8.

This brief example of some of the techniques leaves us with the grid at right.

You should now be able to use what you learned to fill in CN followed by BL, then HL followed by DL and FL.

As you keep going through this puzzle, you'll find it gets easier as you fill in more. And as you keep working through the puzzles in this book, you'll find it gets easier and more fun each time. The final answer is shown here.

—Michael Rios

	A	B	C	D	E	F	G	H	I
J	4	2							
K					2		1	8	4
L	9		5		7		2		6
M	1		4	3	9	2		7	8
N	2	9		7	5	6			
O		7		1	4	8	9		2
P	3		2		6		8		5
Q	8	4	9		3				
R									

	A	B	C	D	E	F	G	H	I
J	4	2	1	6	8	3	5	9	7
K	7	3	6	5	2	9	1	8	4
L	9	8	5	4	7	1	2	3	6
M	1	5	4	3	9	2	6	7	8
N	2	9	8	7	5	6	4	1	3
O	6	7	3	1	4	8	9	5	2
P	3	1	2	9	6	7	8	4	5
Q	8	4	9	2	3	5	7	6	1
R	5	6	7	8	1	4	3	2	9

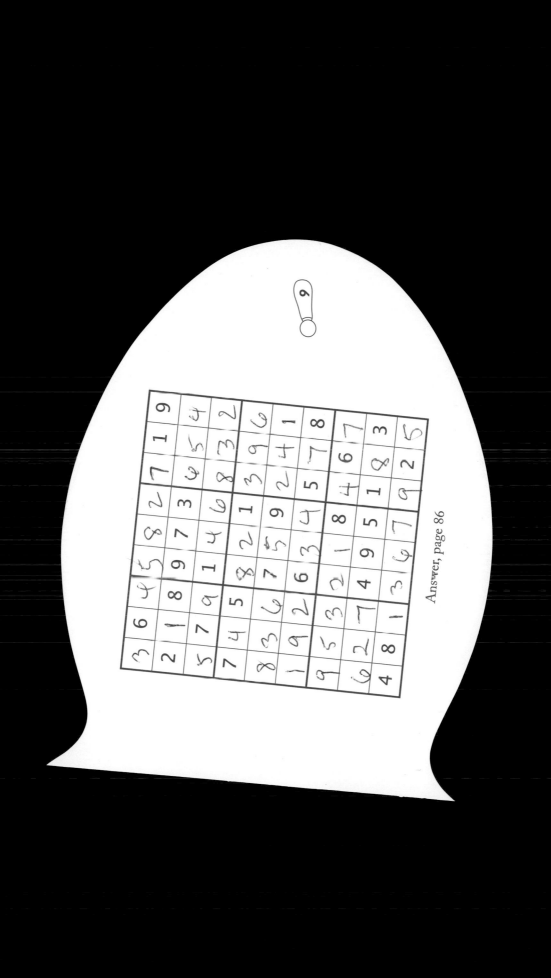

Answer, page 86

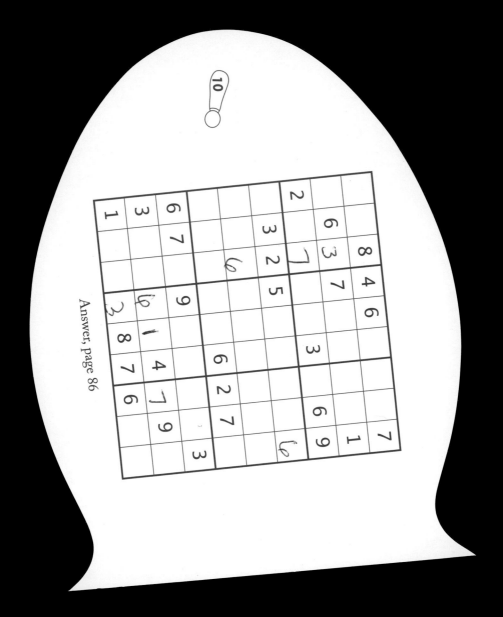

10

2		6	3	8	4	6		7
				7			1	
	3	2	7	5		3		9
			6				6	
6		9		6	2	7		6
3	7		6	1	4	7	9	3
1		3	8	7	6			

Answer, page 86

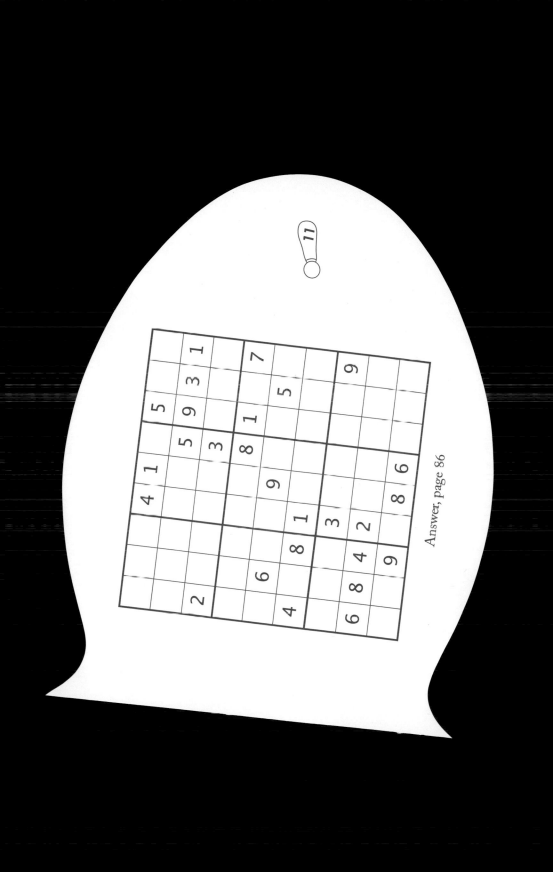

11

Answer, page 86

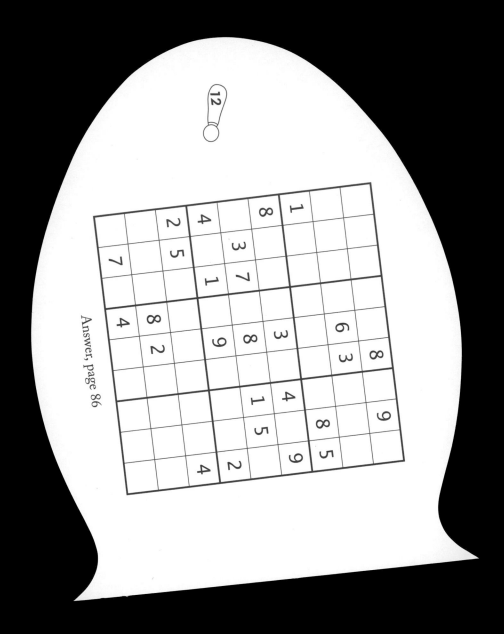

12

Answer, page 86

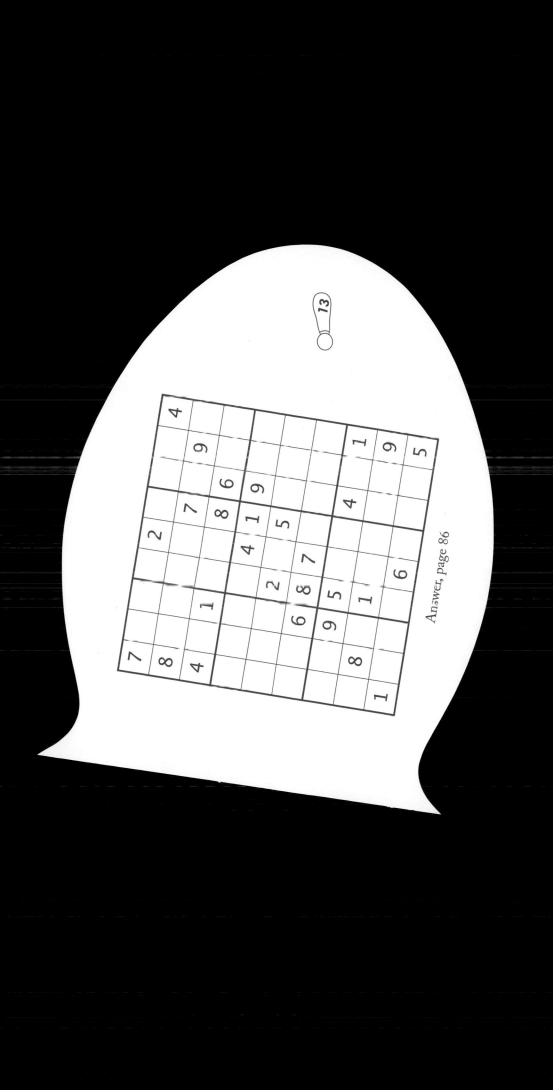

13

Answer, page 86

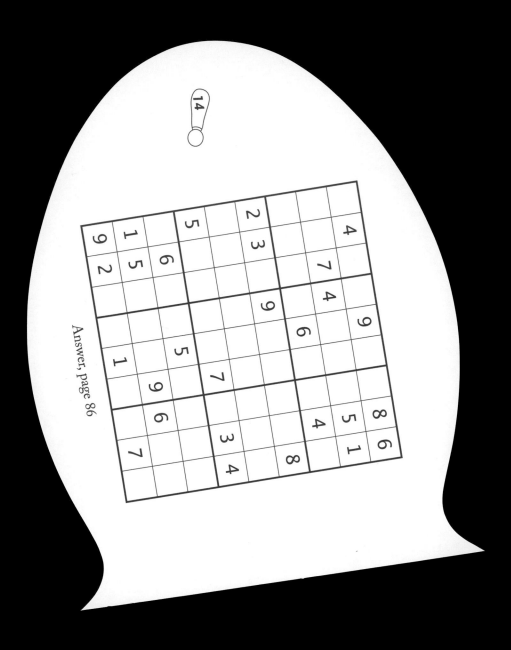

14

Answer, page 86

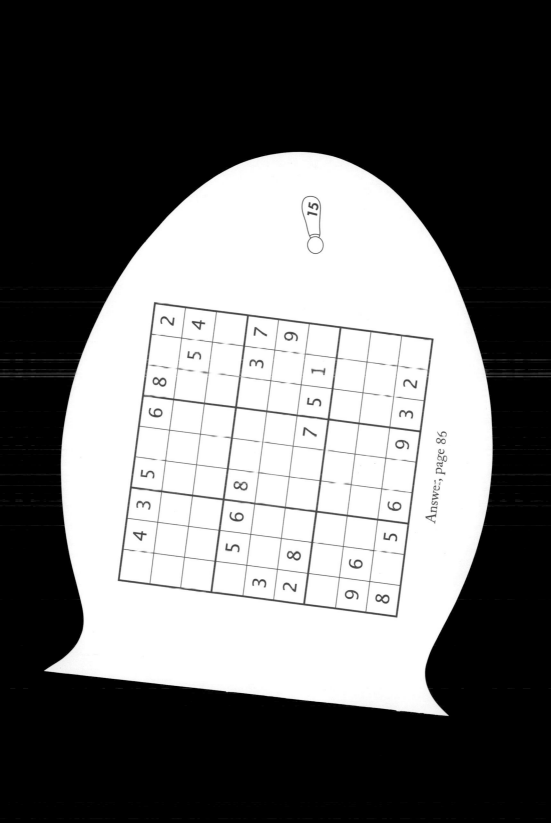

15

Answers, page 86

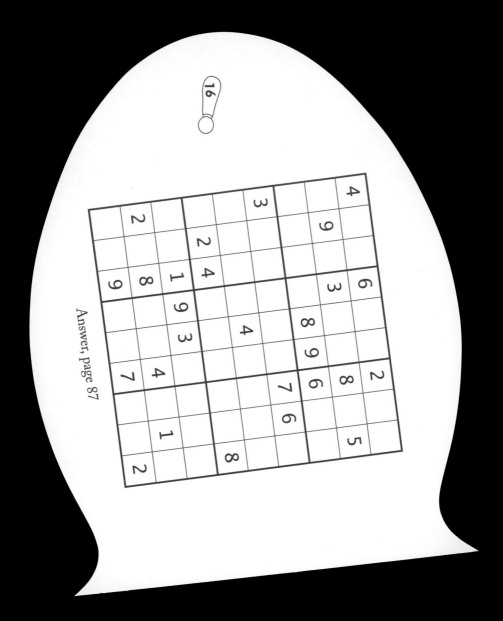

Answer, page 87

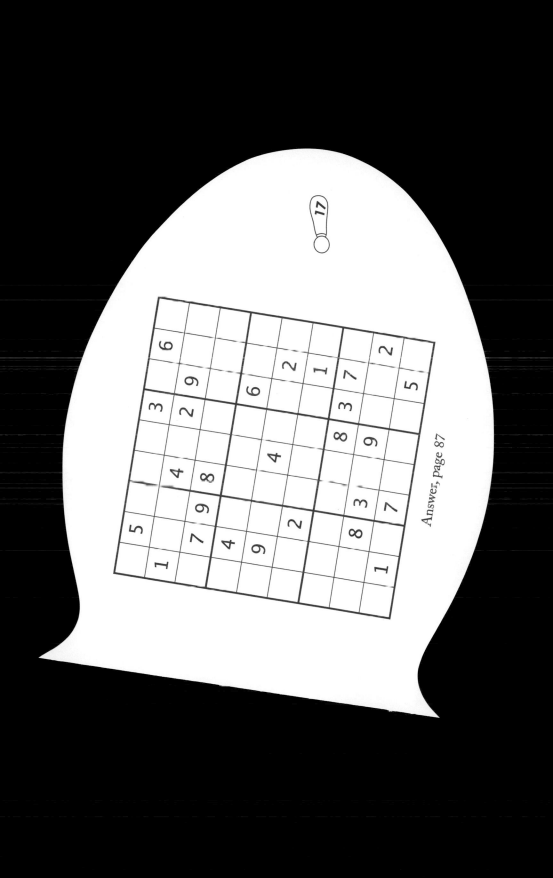

17

Answer, page 87

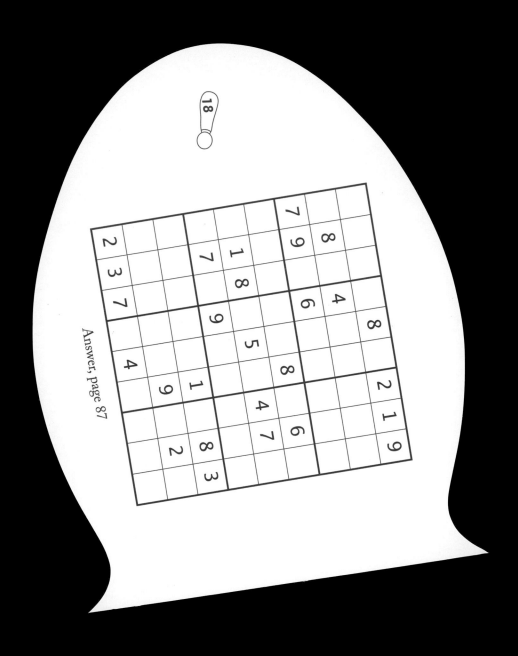

18

Answer, page 87

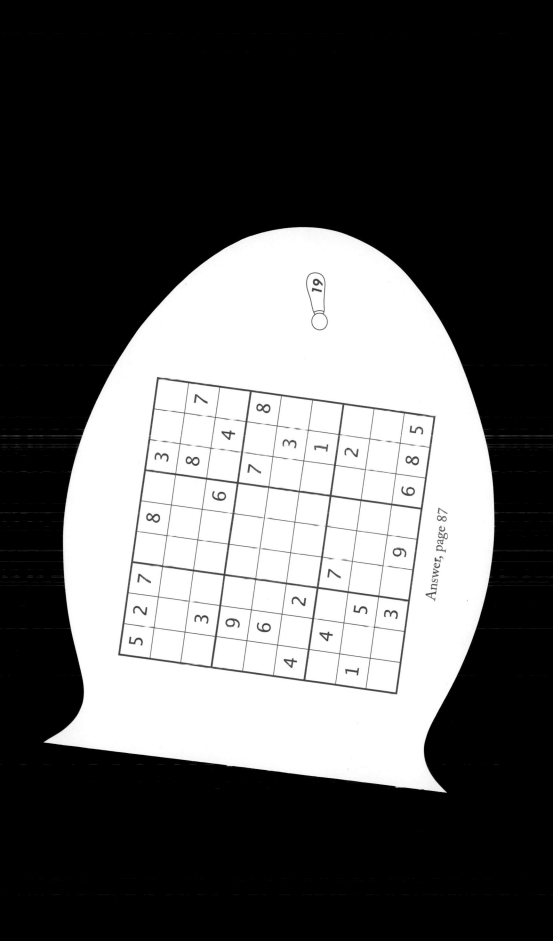

19

Answer, page 87

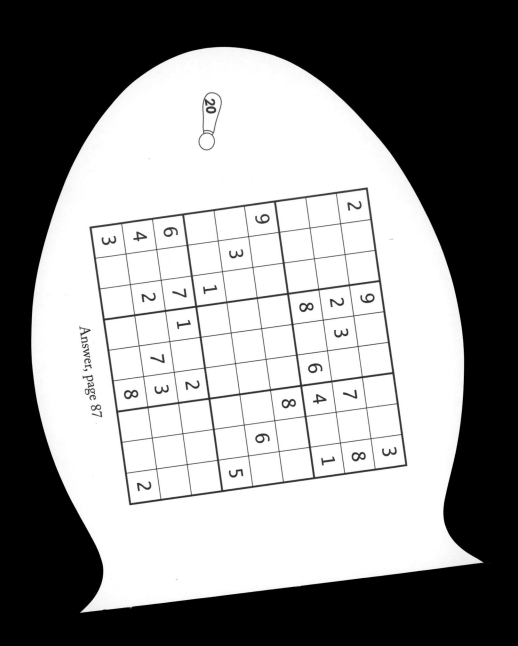

20

Answer, page 87

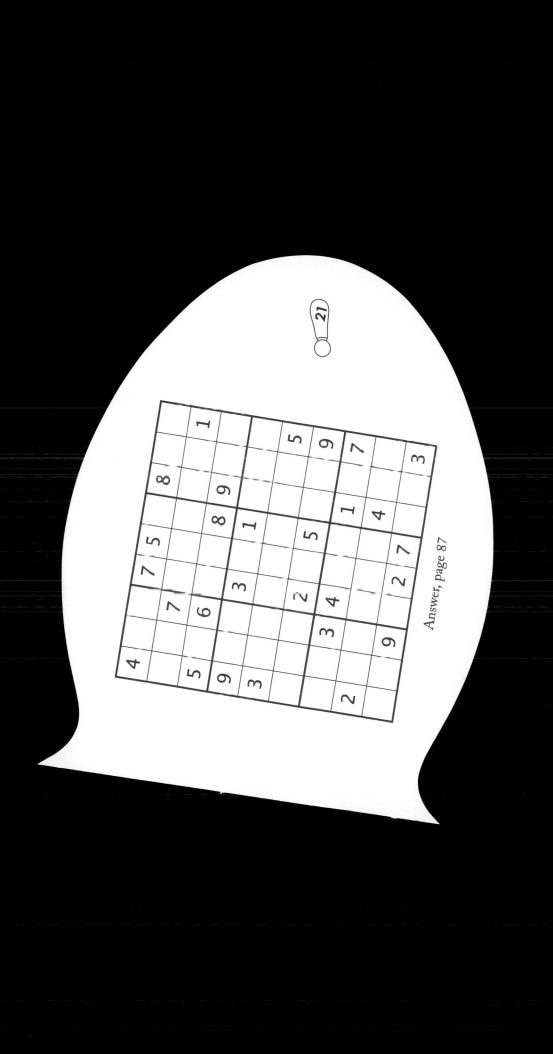

21

Answer, page 87

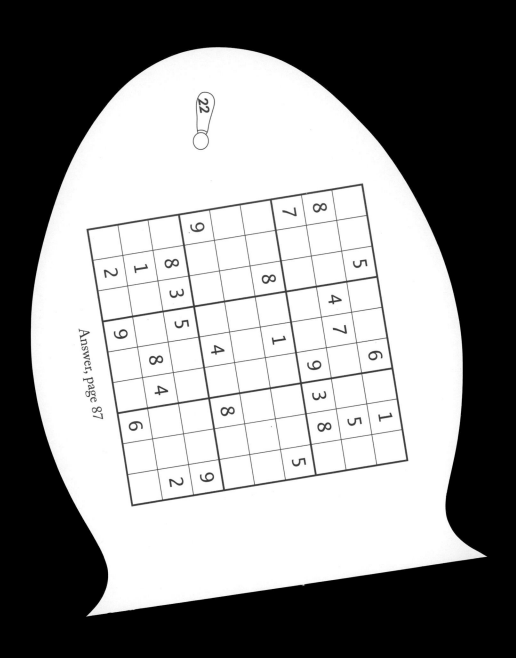

Answer, page 87

22

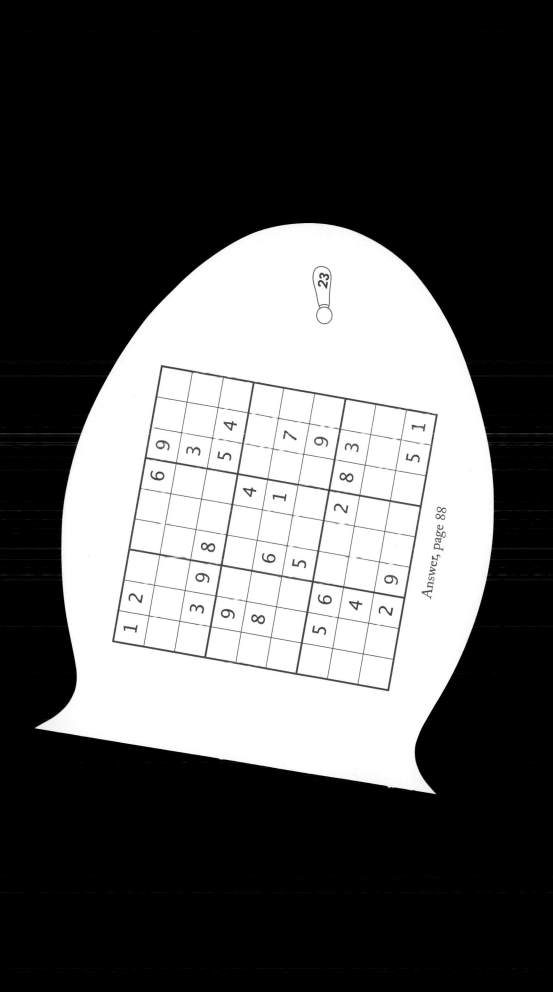

23

Answer, page 88

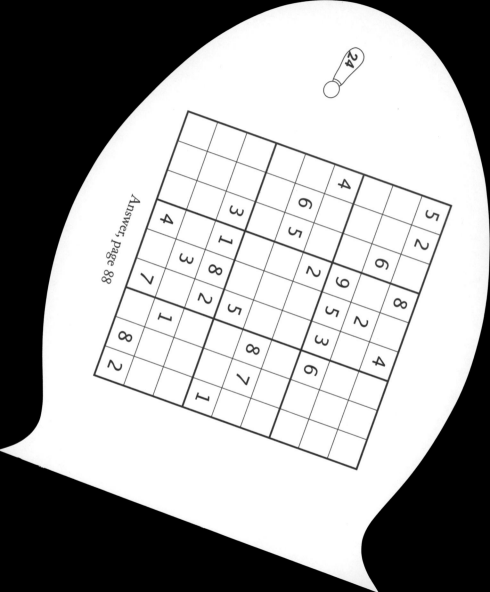

Answer, page 88

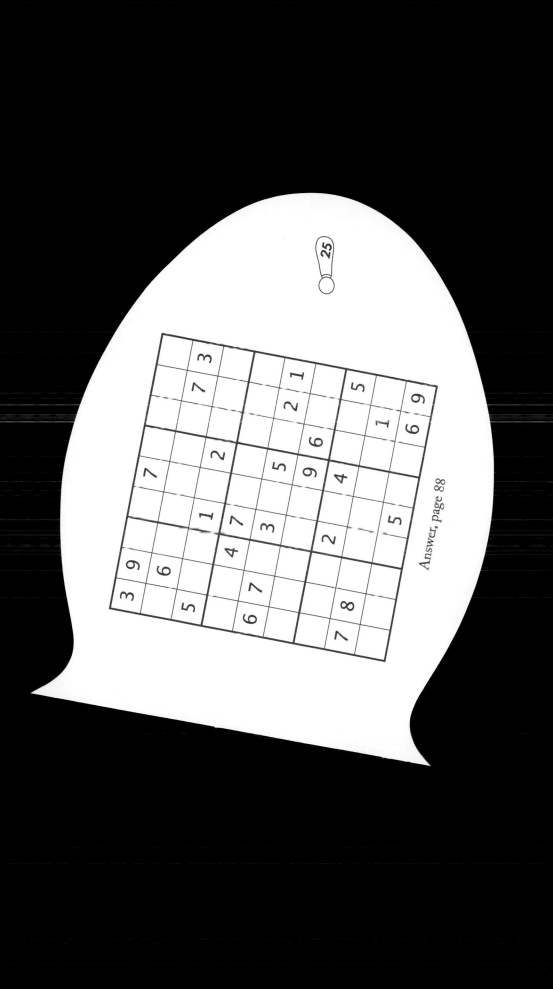

Answer, page 88

25

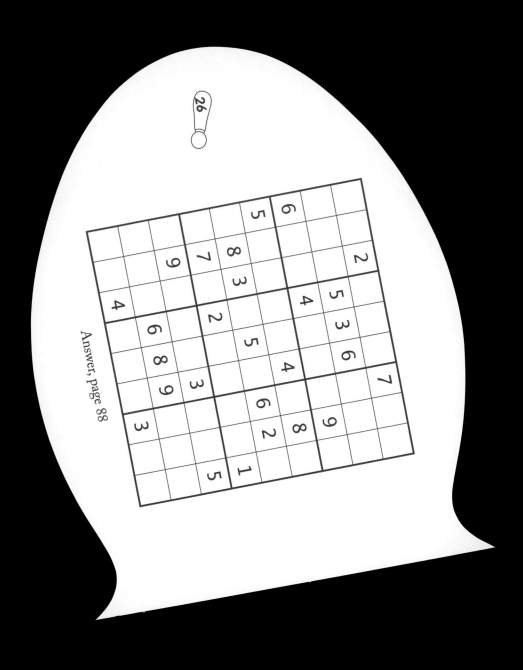

26

Answer, page 88

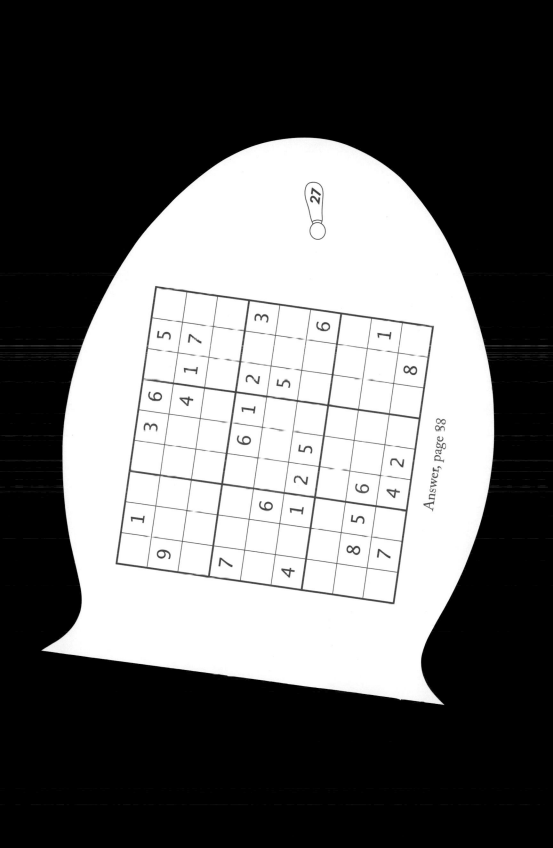

27

			3		6		1	
5	1		2					8
7	4	6	5					
		3	1					
			6	5			6	2
1			2		6	5	4	
			1	2		8	7	
9	7		4					

Answer, page 88

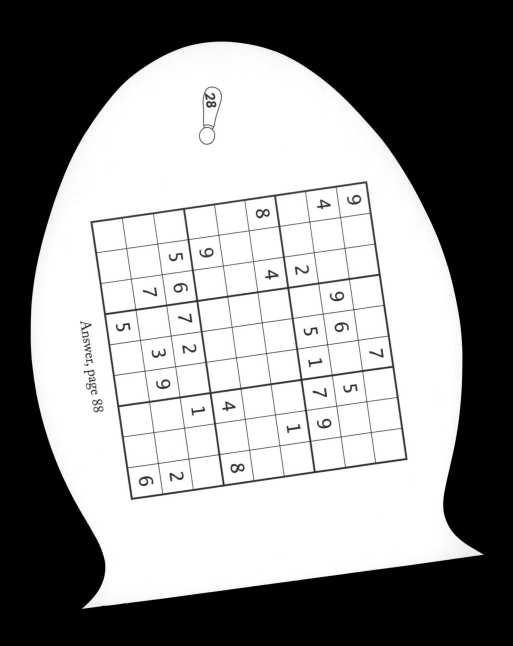

Answer, page 88

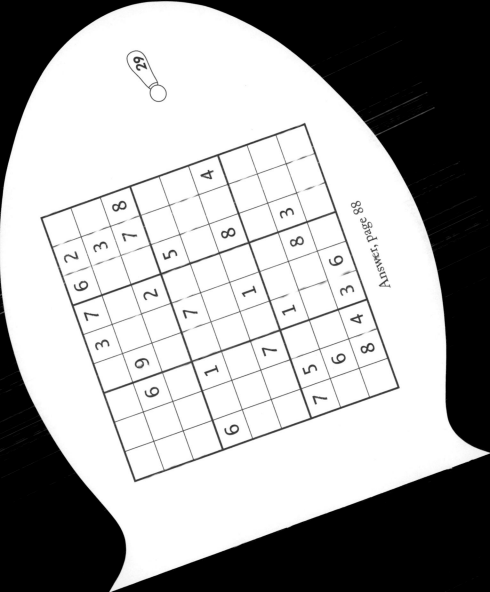

29

Answer, page 88

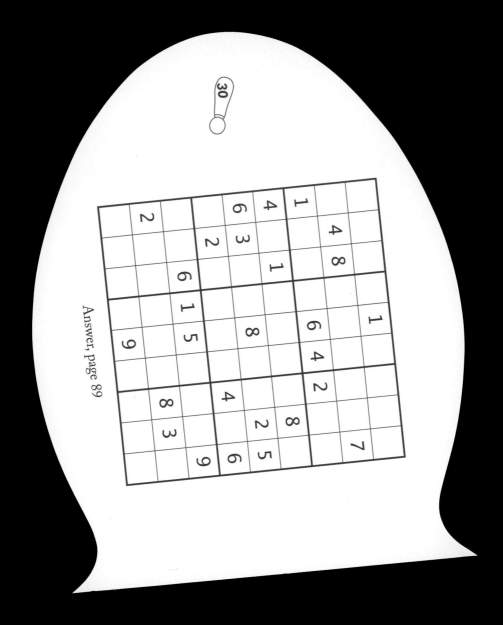

Answer, page 89

30

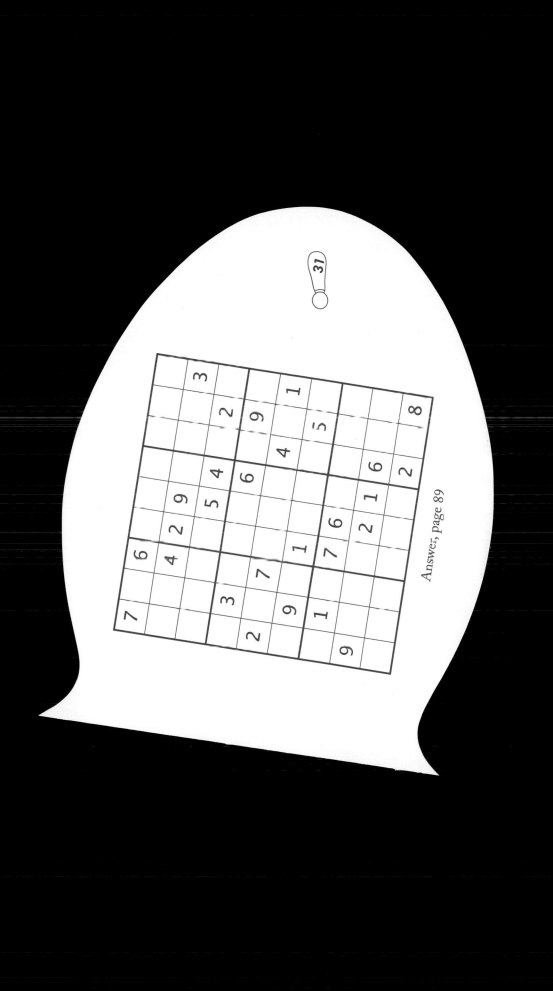

31

Answer, page 89

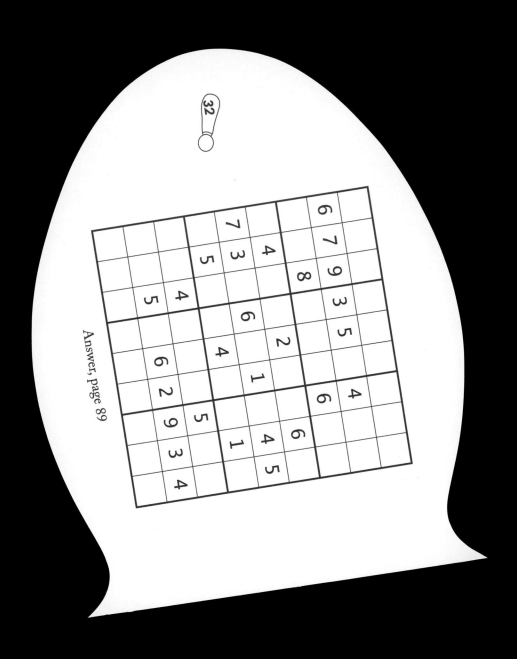

32

Answer, page 89

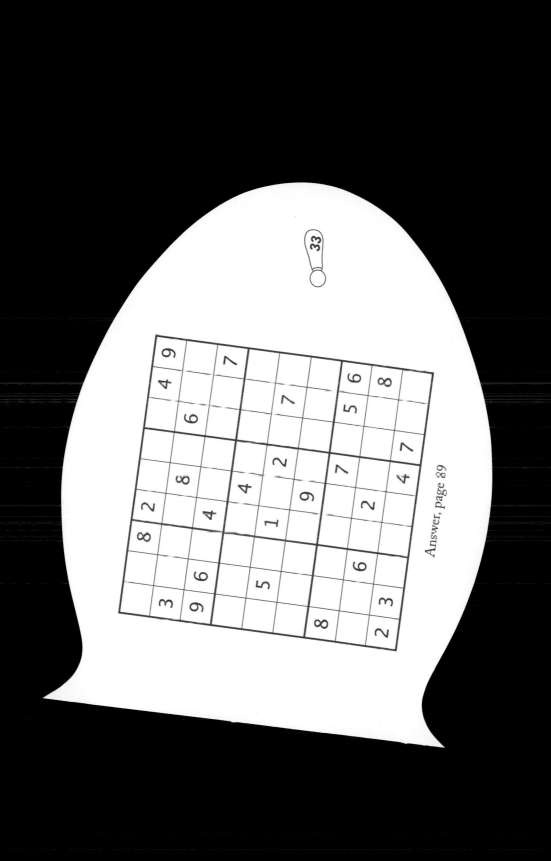

33

Answer, page 89

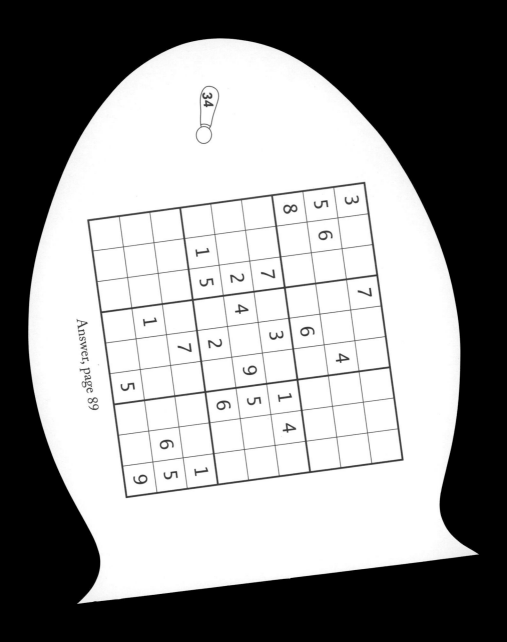

Answer, page 89

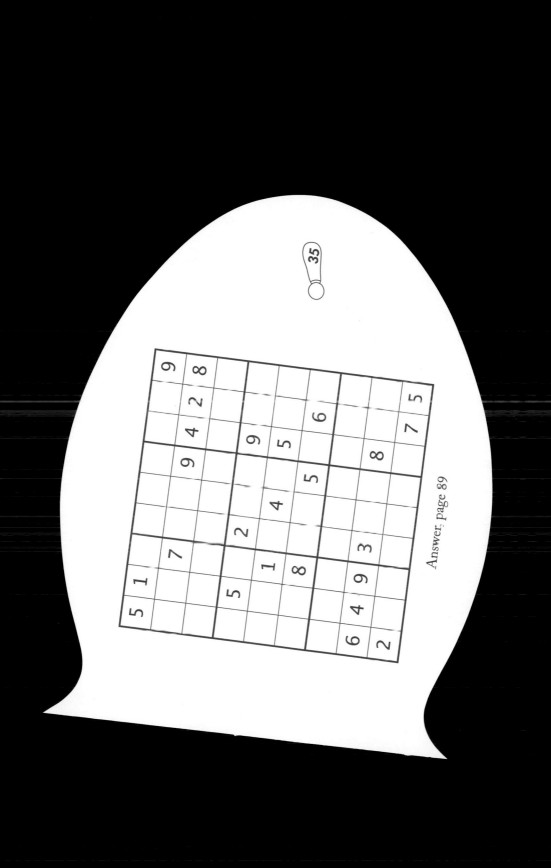

Answer, page 89

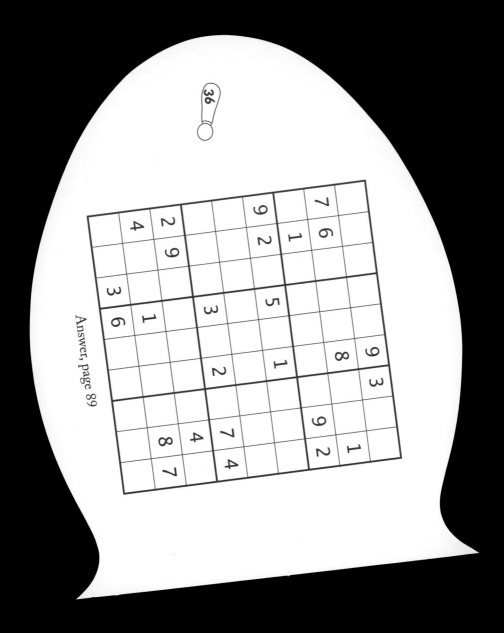

36

Answer, page 89

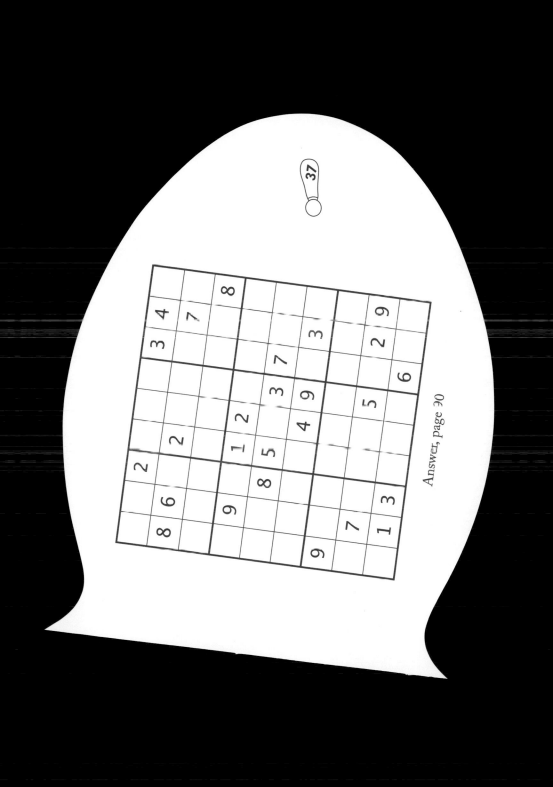

37

Answer, page 90

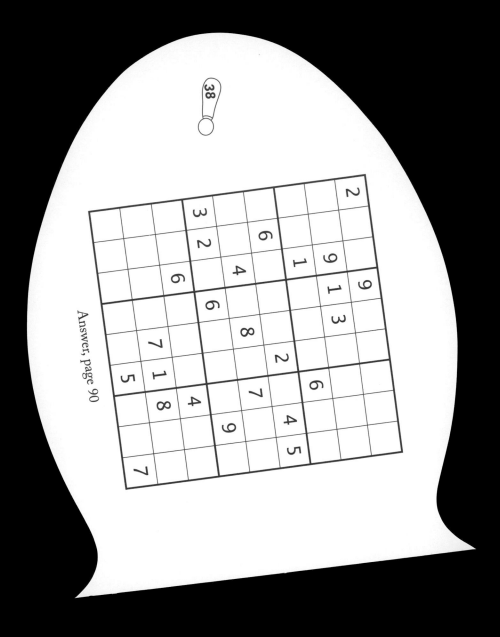

Answer, page 90

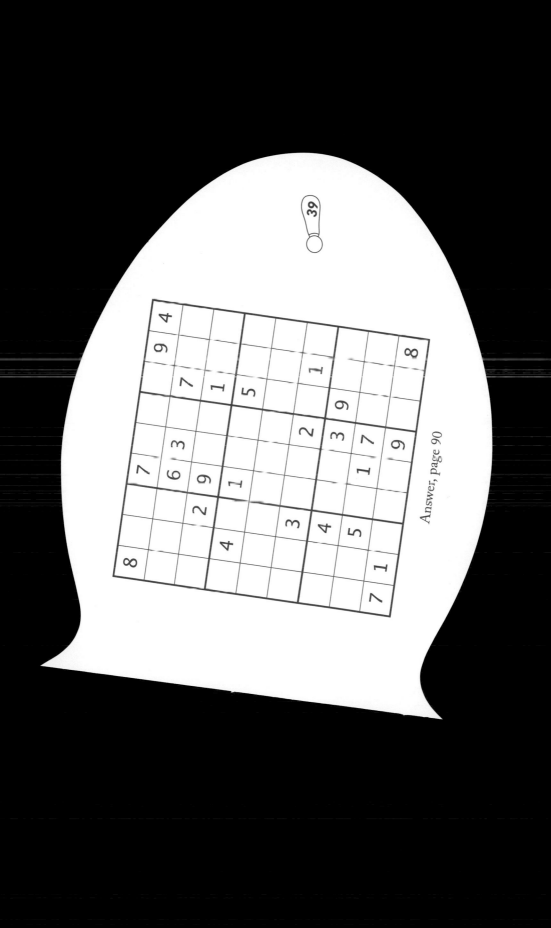

39

Answer, page 90

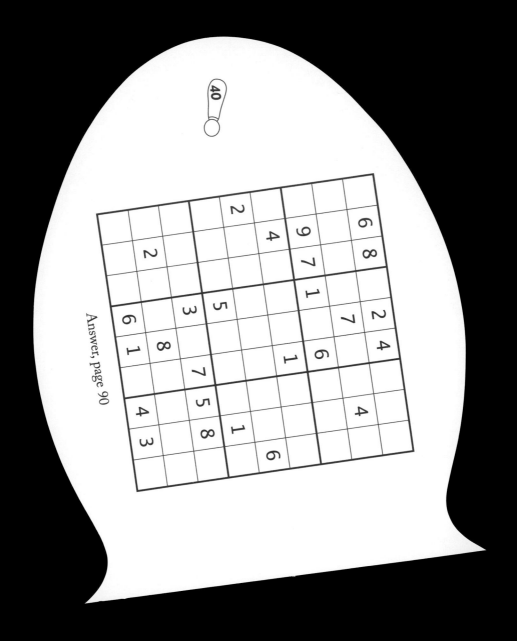

40

Answer, page 90

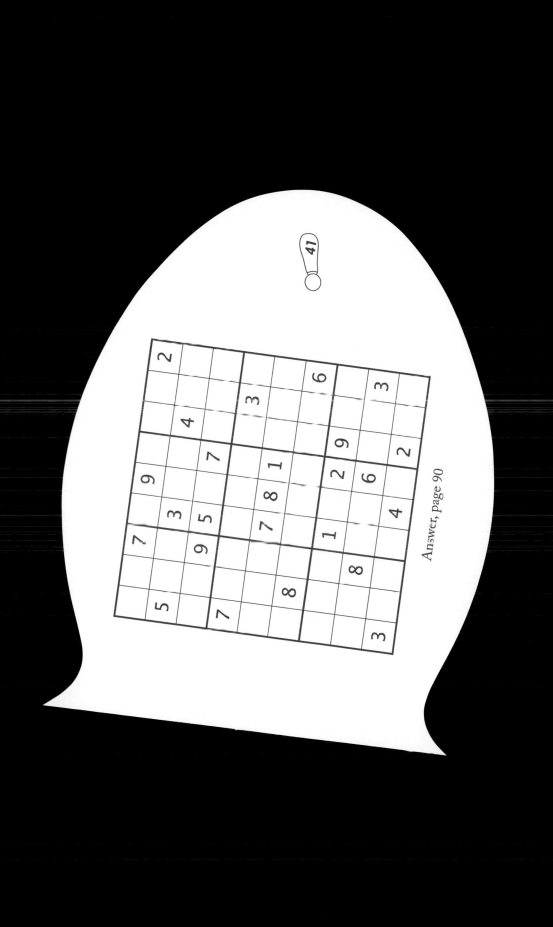

41

Answer, page 90

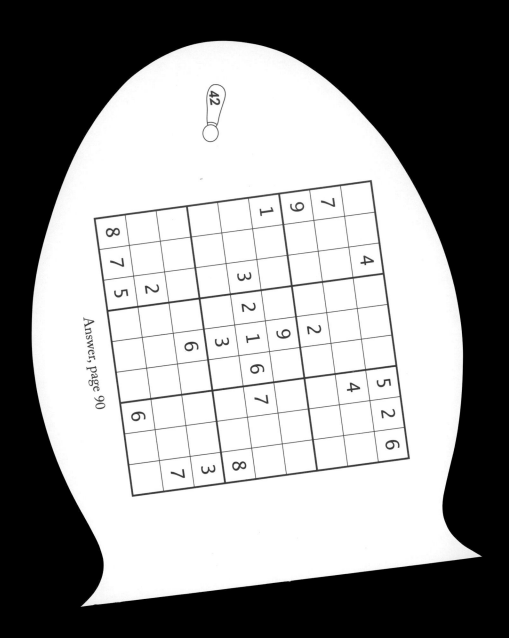

Answer, page 90

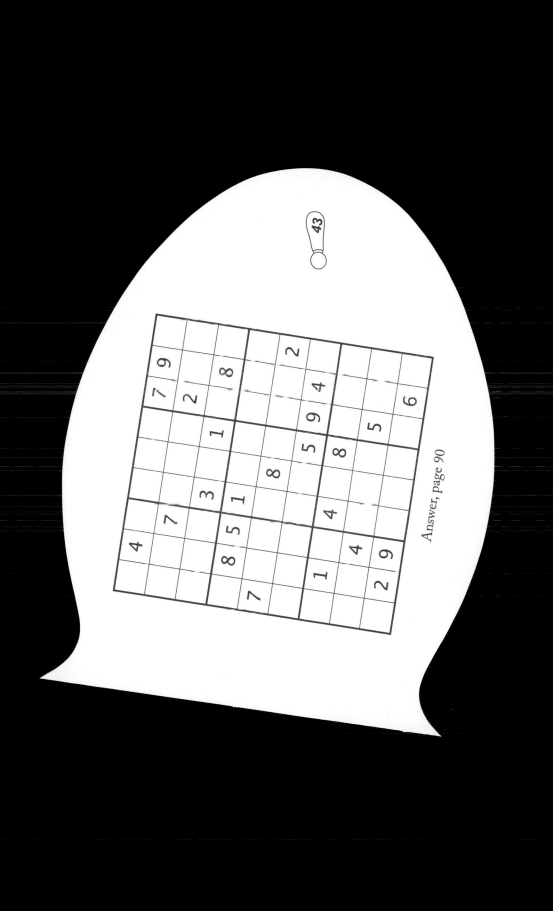

43

Answer, page 90

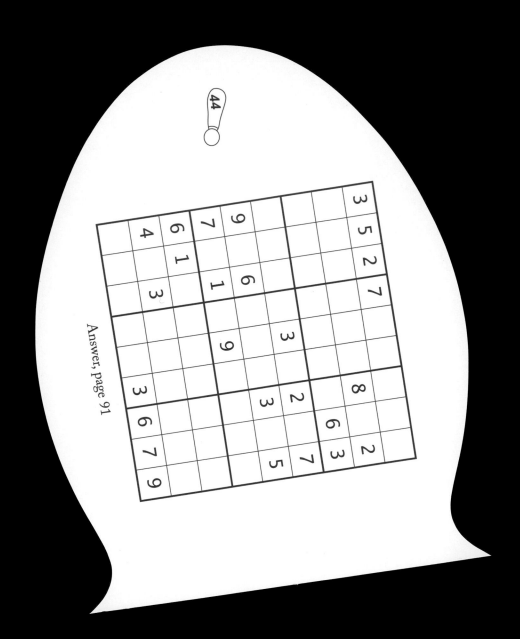

44

Answer, page 91

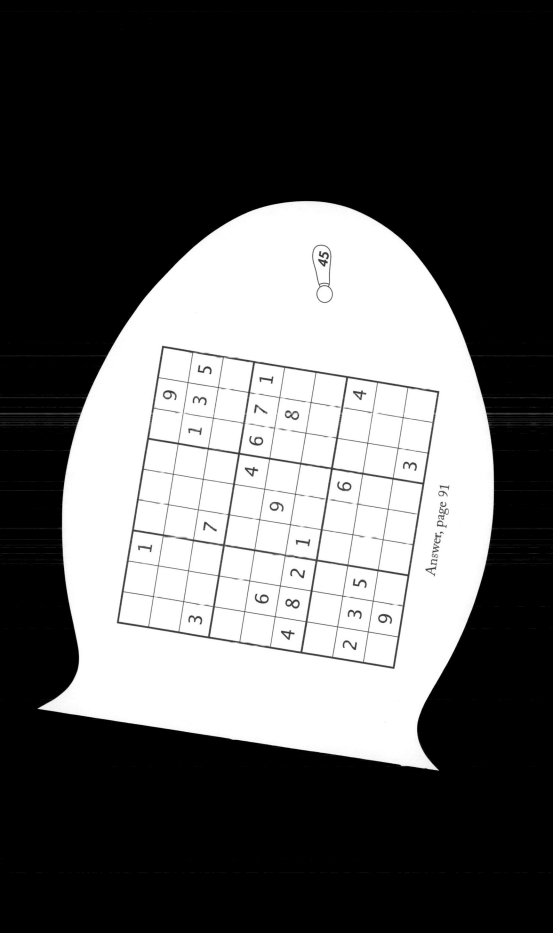

45

Answer, page 91

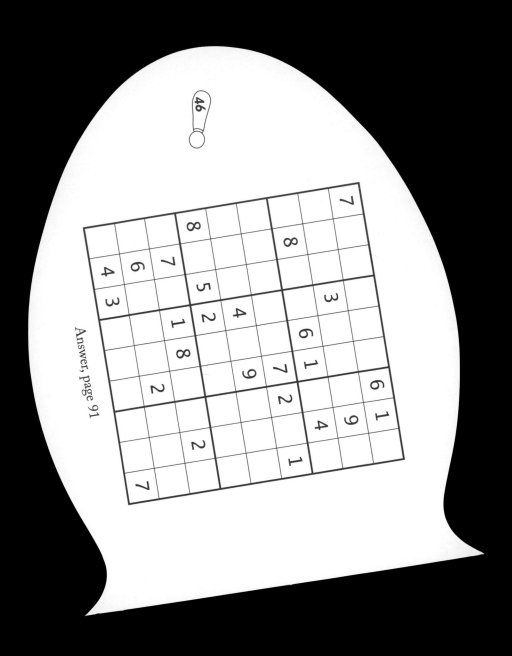

46

Answer, page 91

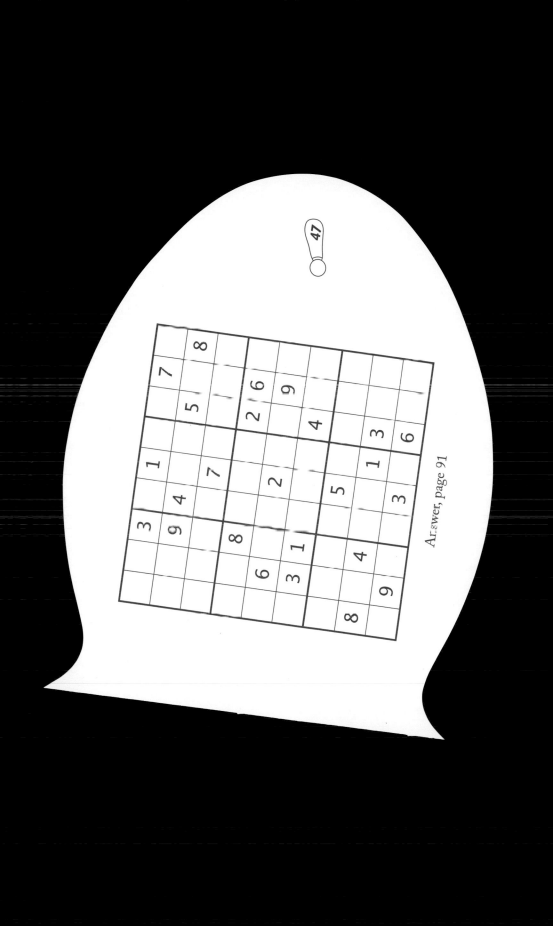

47

Answer, page 91

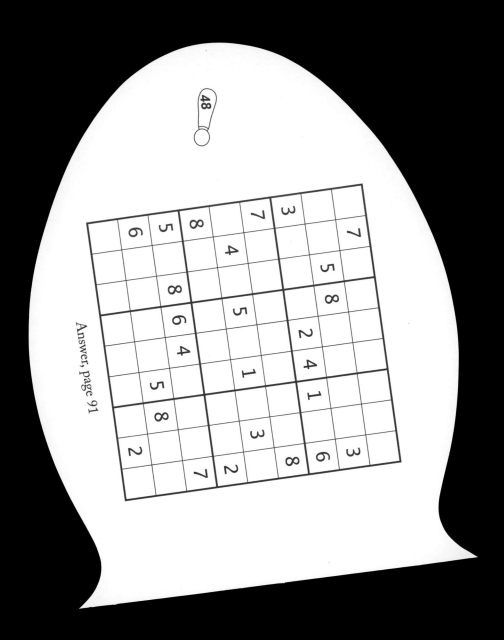

48

Answer, page 91

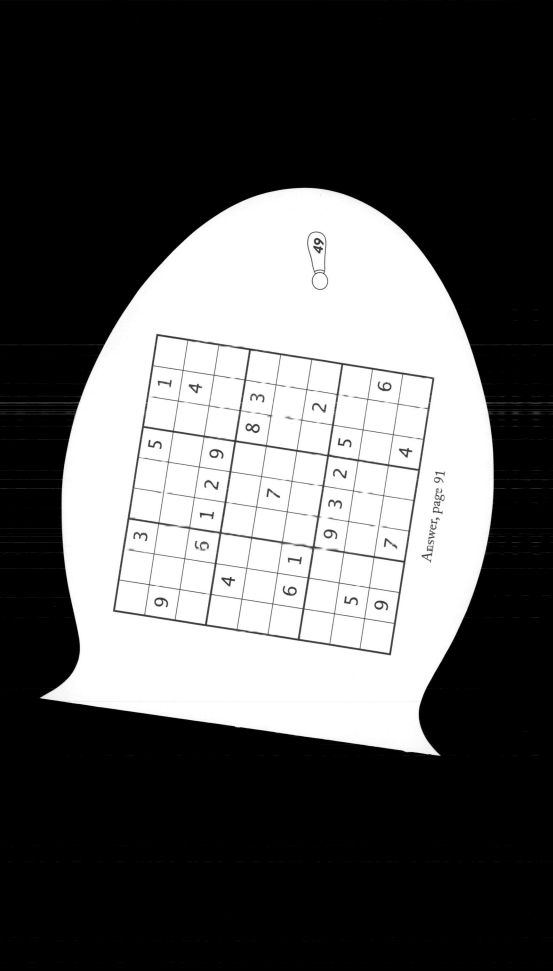

49

Answer, page 91

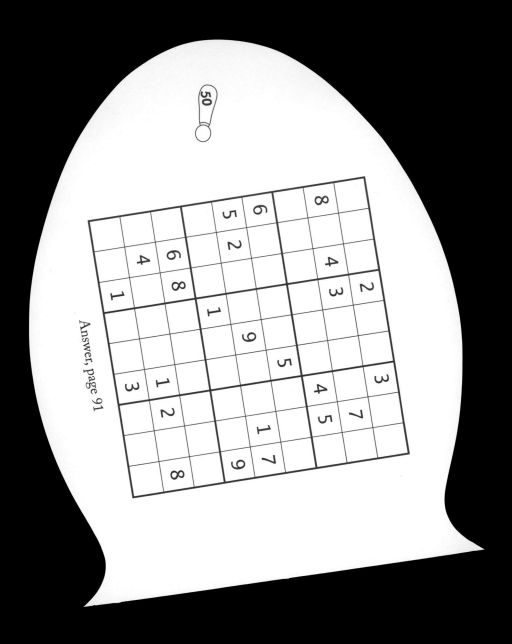

Answer, page 91

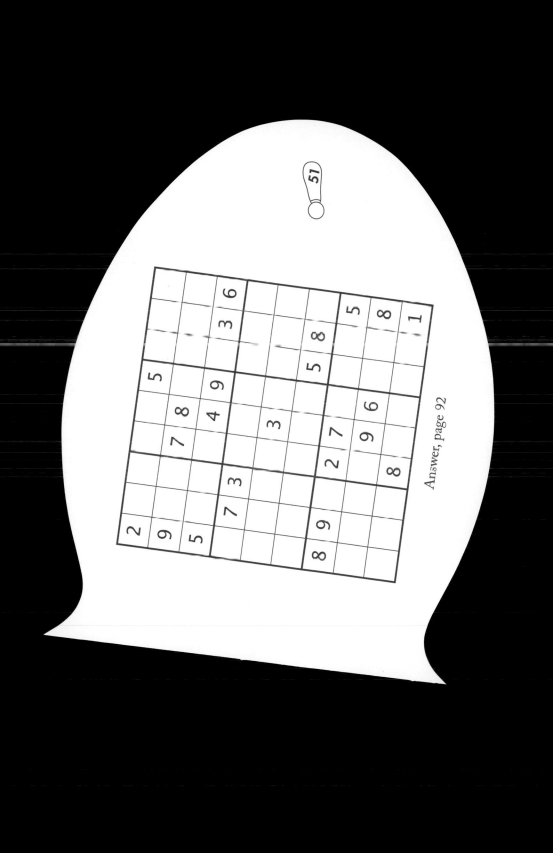

51

Answer, page 92

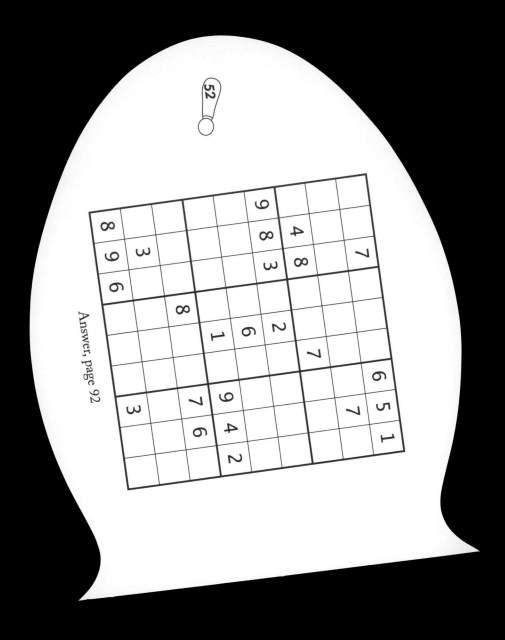

Answer, page 92

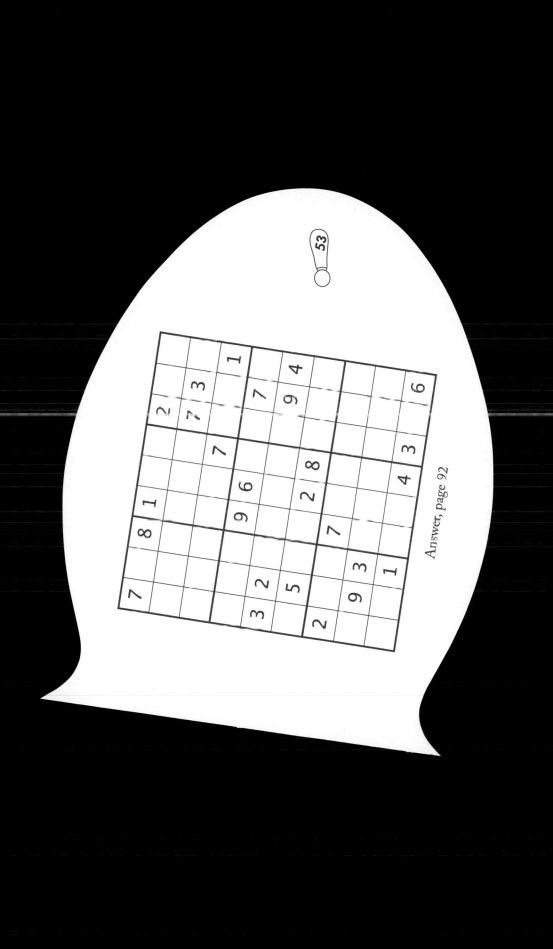

53

Answer, page 92

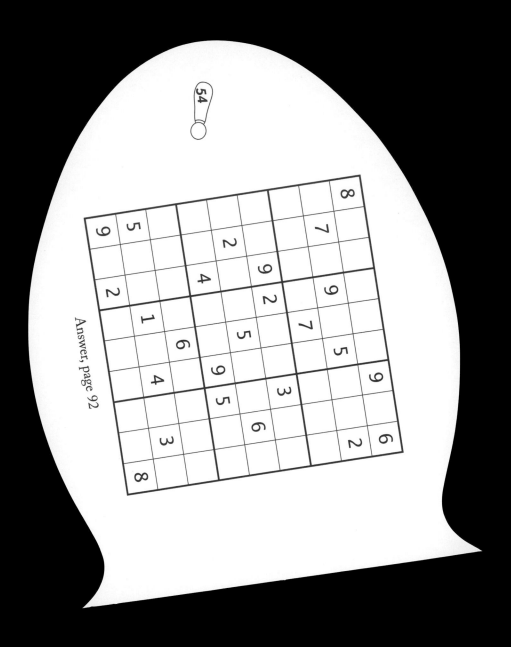

Answer, page 92

54

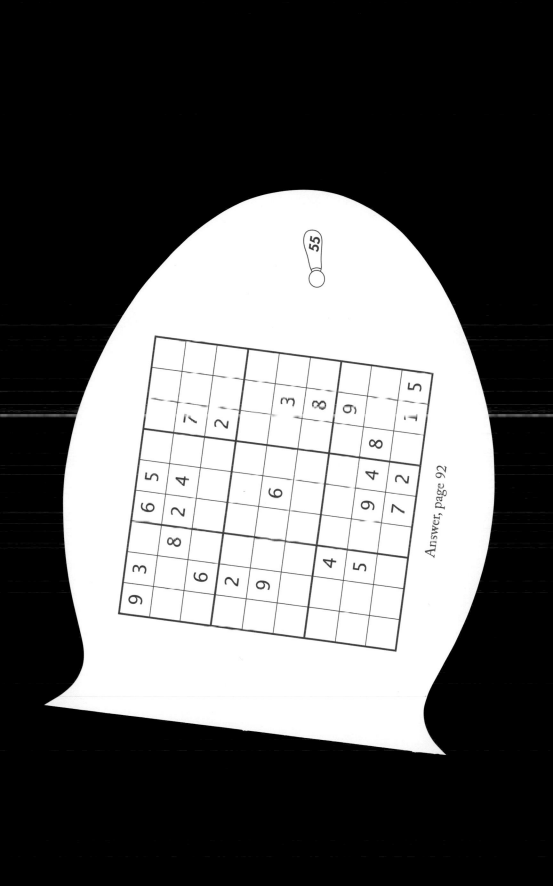

55

Answer, page 92

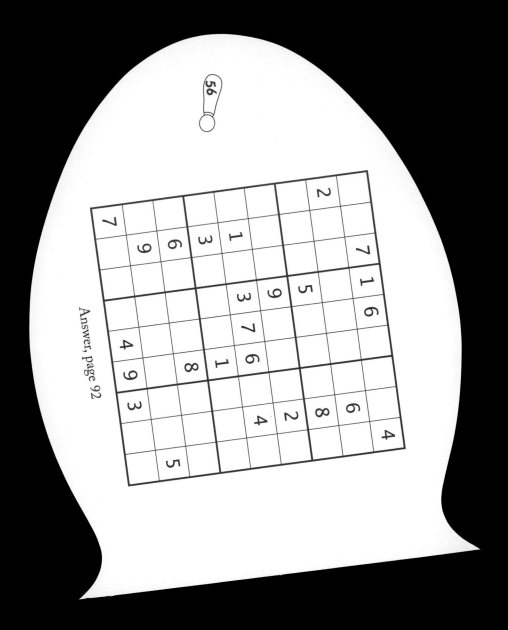

Answer, page 92

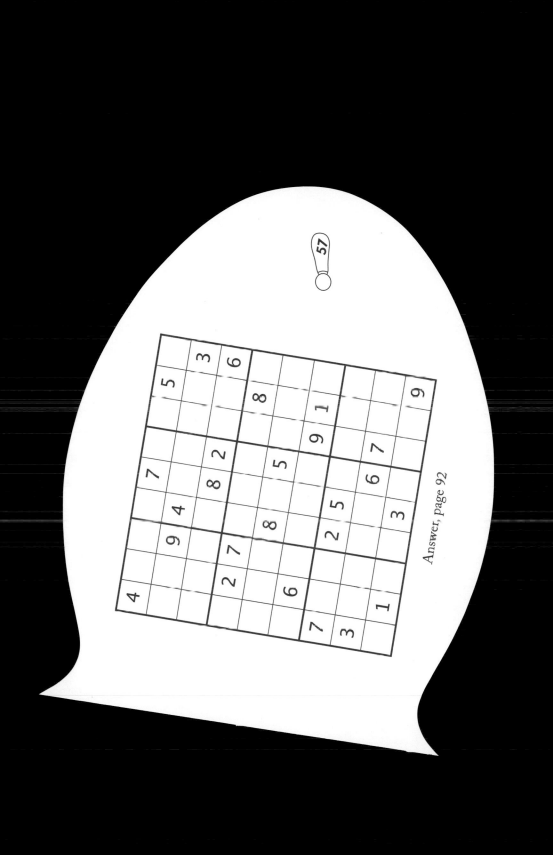

57

Answer, page 92

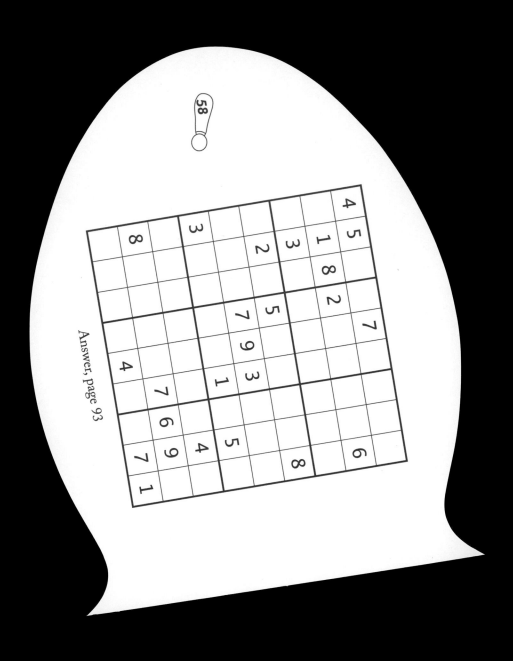

58

Answer, page 93

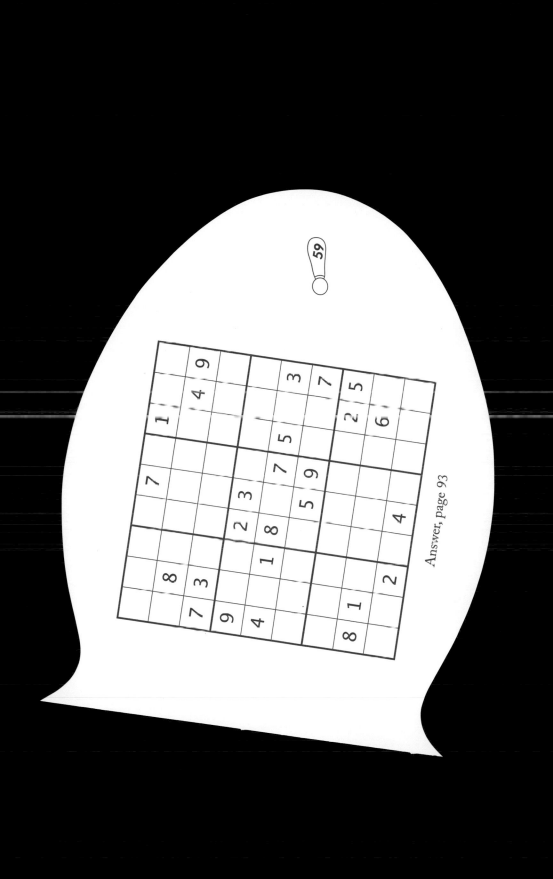

59

Answer, page 93

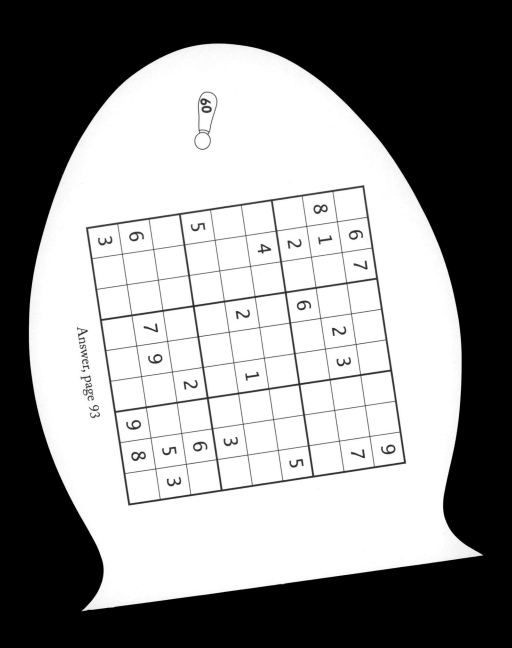

Answer, page 93

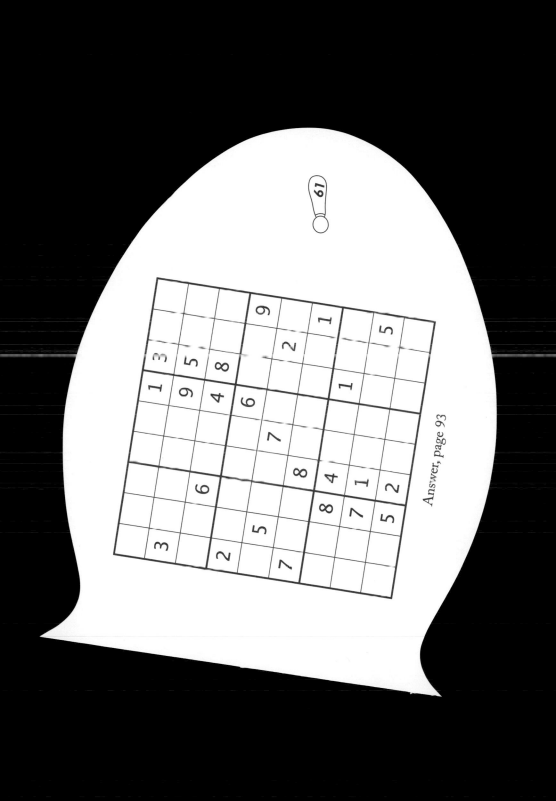

61

Answer, page 93

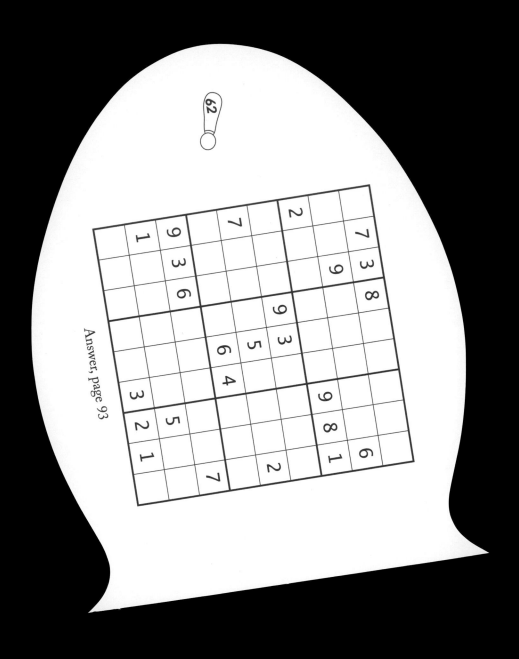

62

Answer, page 93

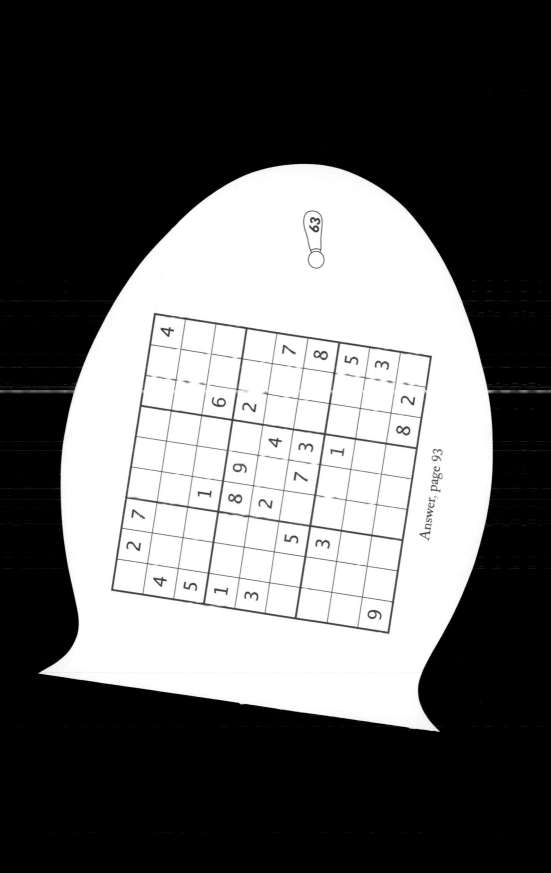

63

Answer, page 93

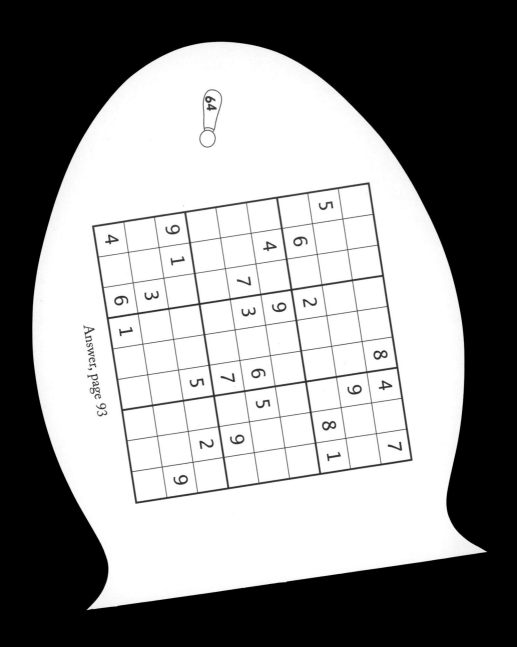

64

Answer, page 93

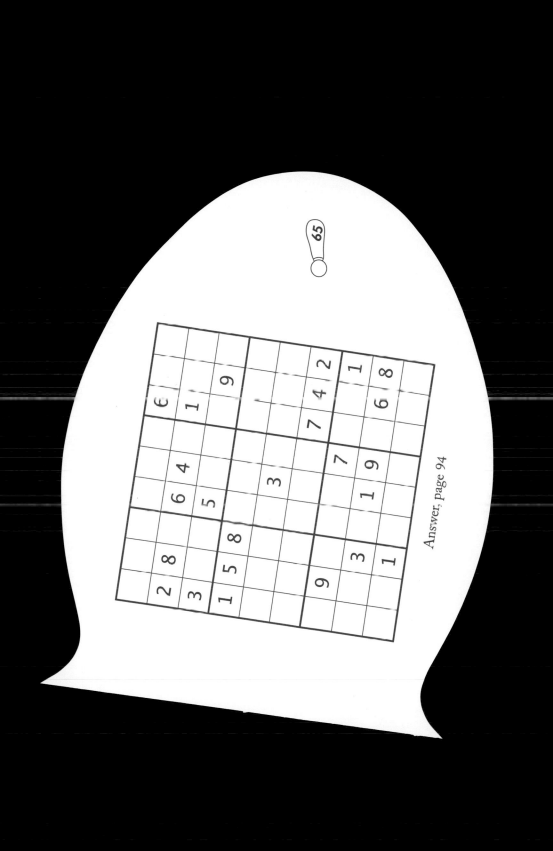

65

Answer, page 94

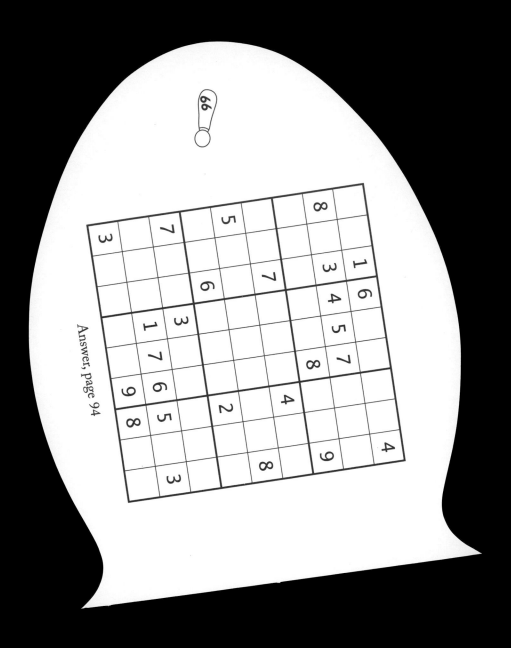

Answer, page 94

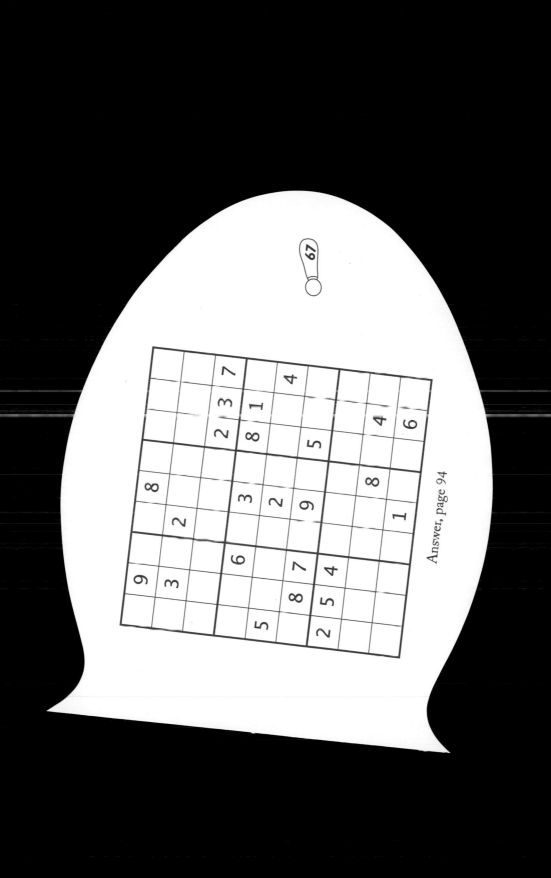

Answer, page 94

67

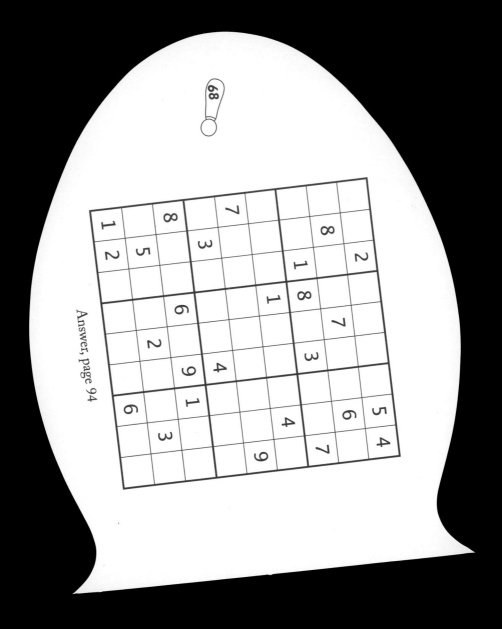

Answer, page 94

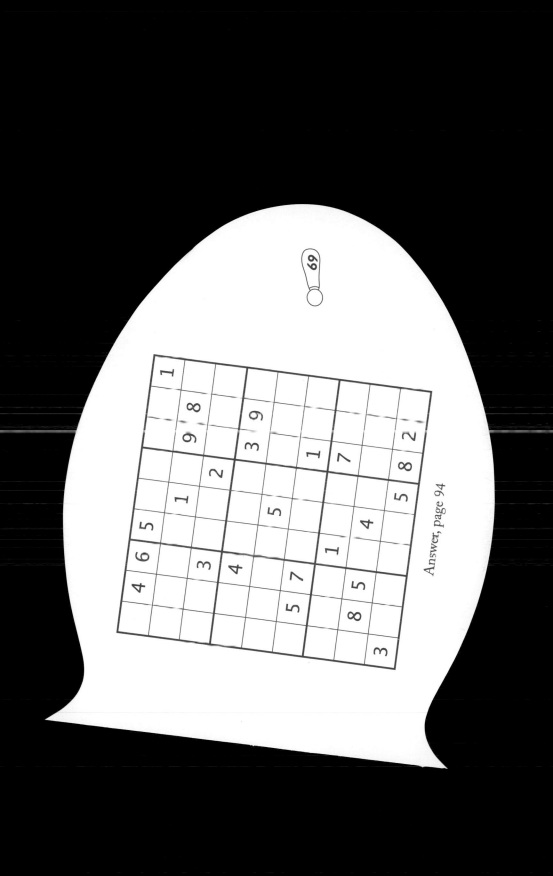

69

Answer, page 94

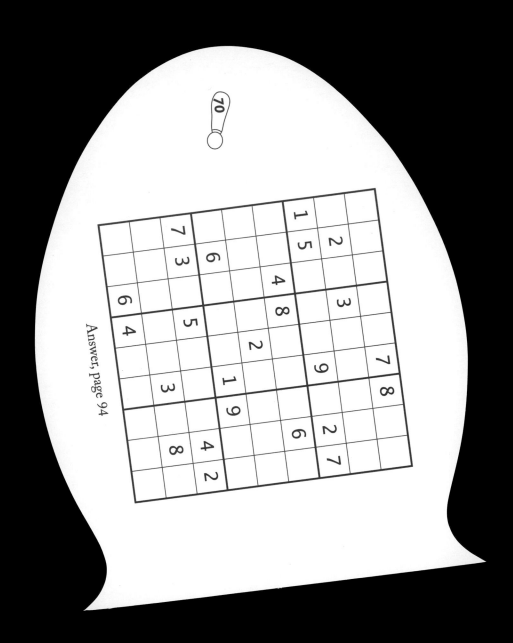

Answer, page 94

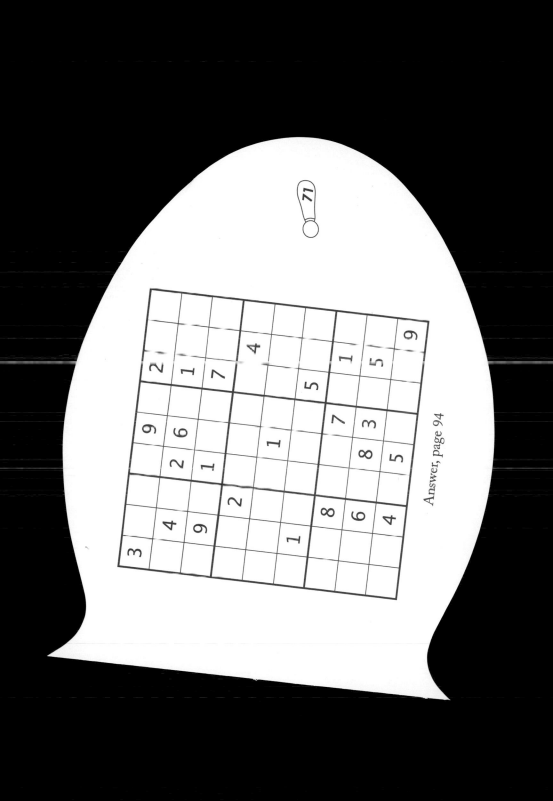

71

Answer, page 94

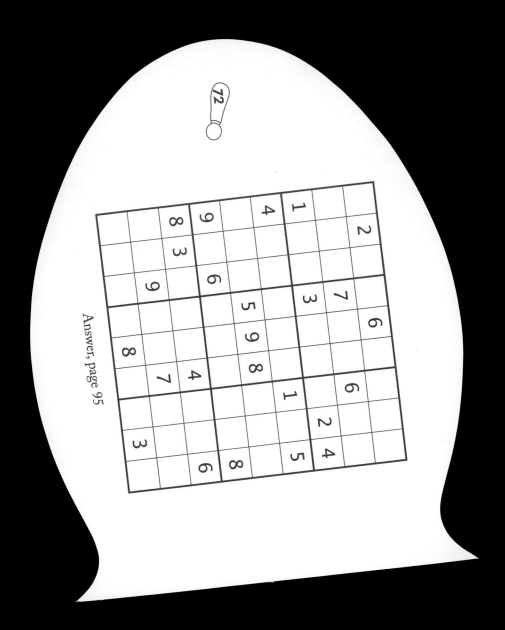

Answer, page 95

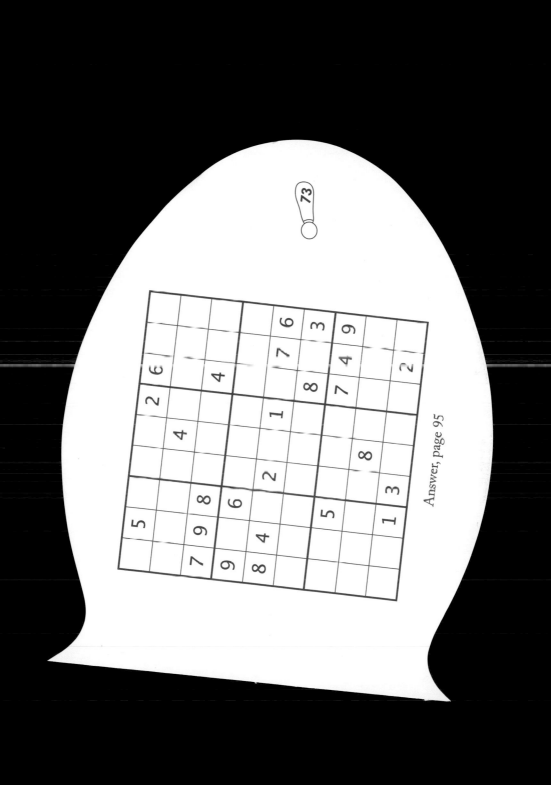

73

Answer, page 95

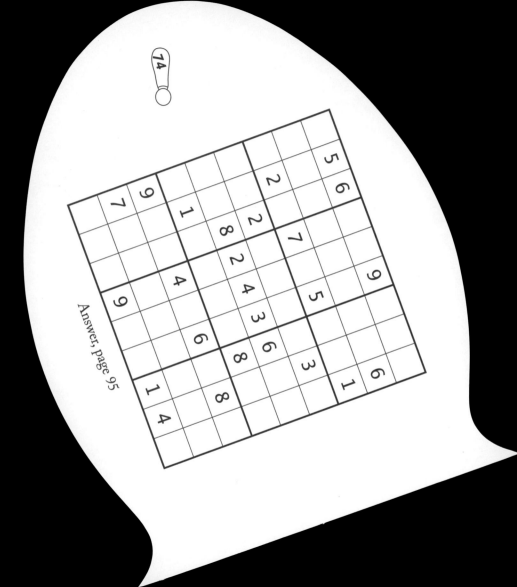

74

Answer, page 95

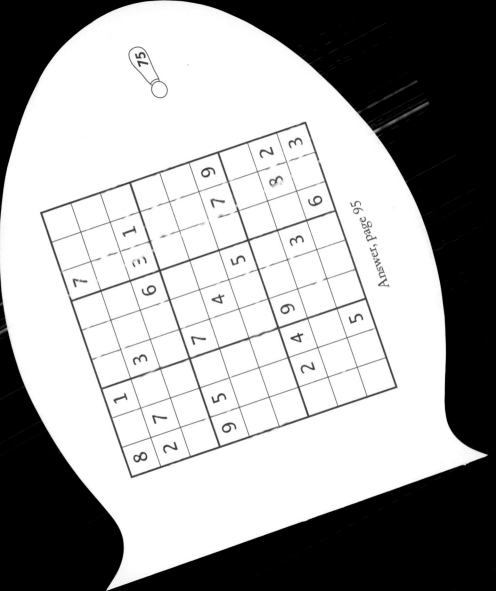

75

Answer, page 95

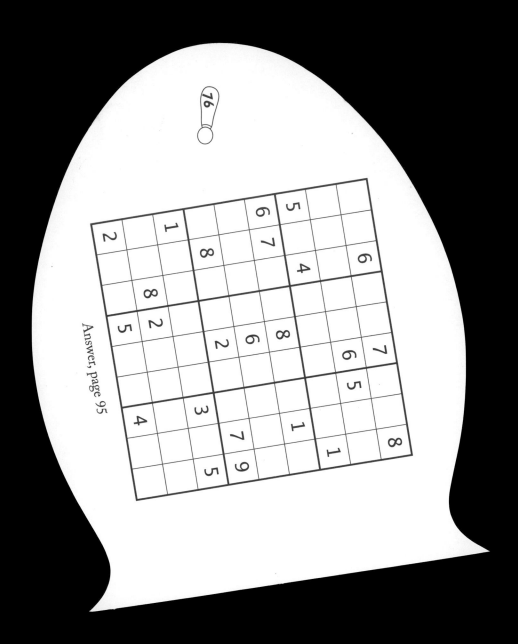

Answer, page 95

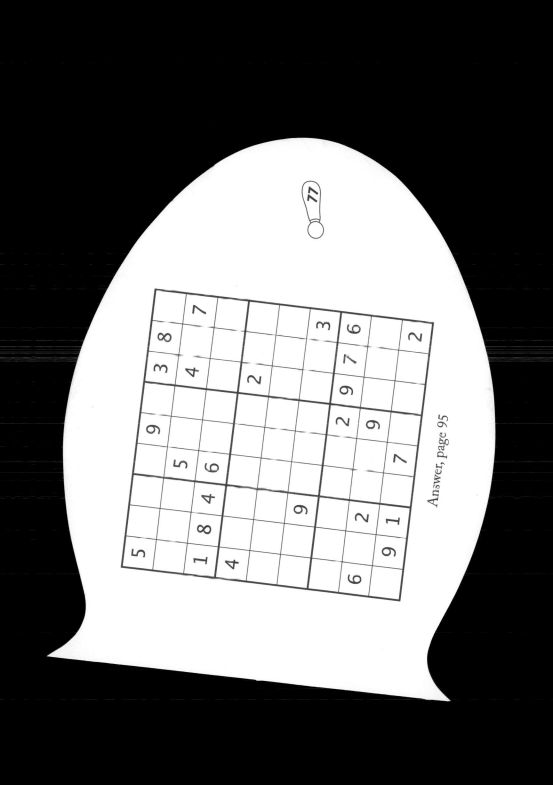

77

Answer, page 95

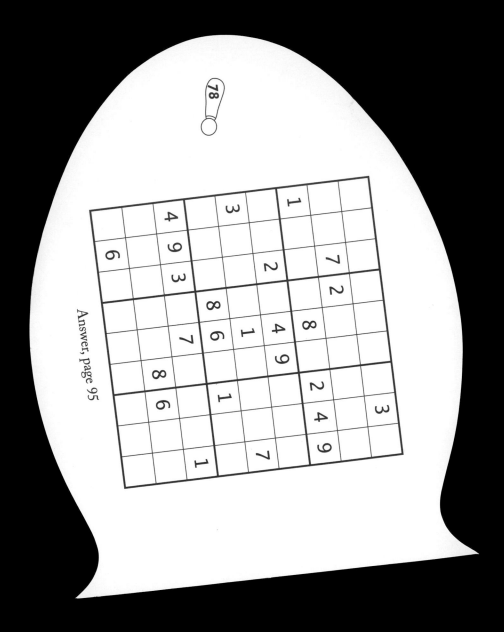

78

Answer, page 95

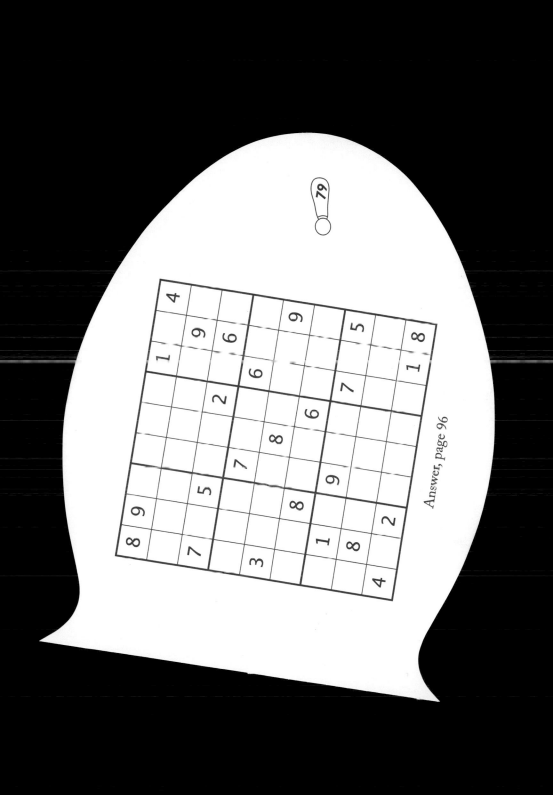

79

Answer, page 96

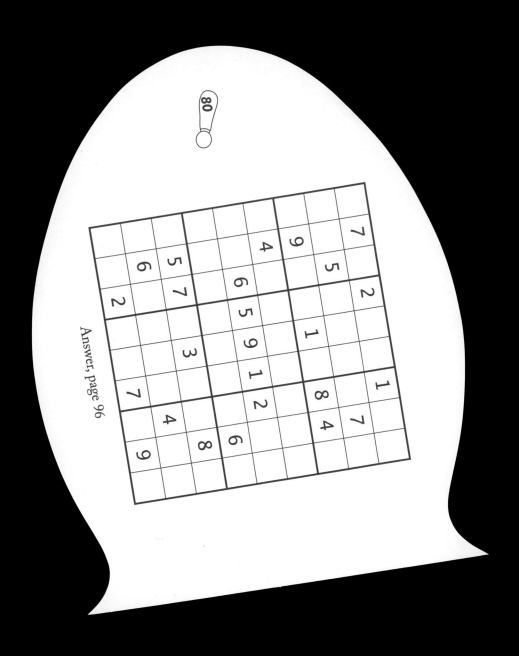

80

Answer, page 96

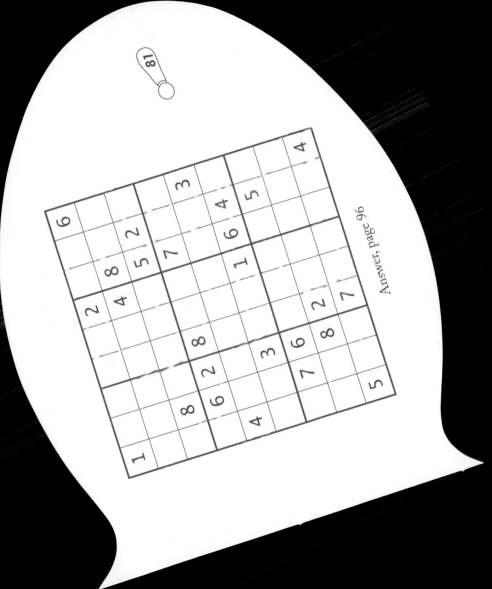

Answer, Page 96

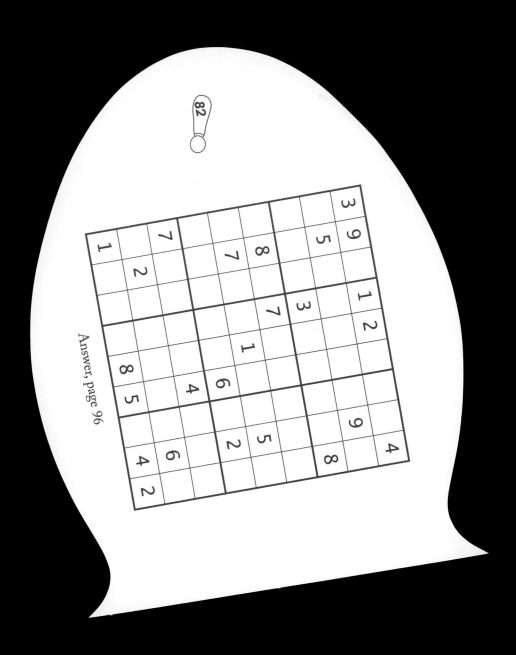

82

Answer, page 96

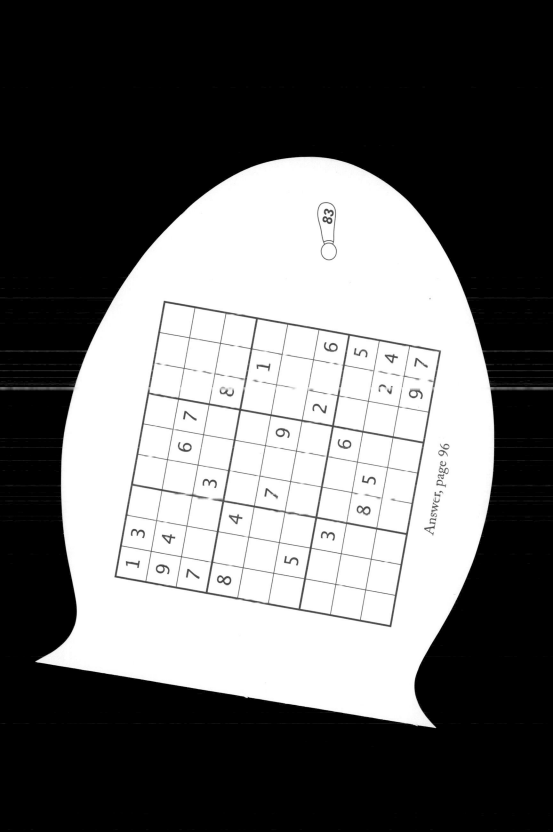

83

Answer, page 96

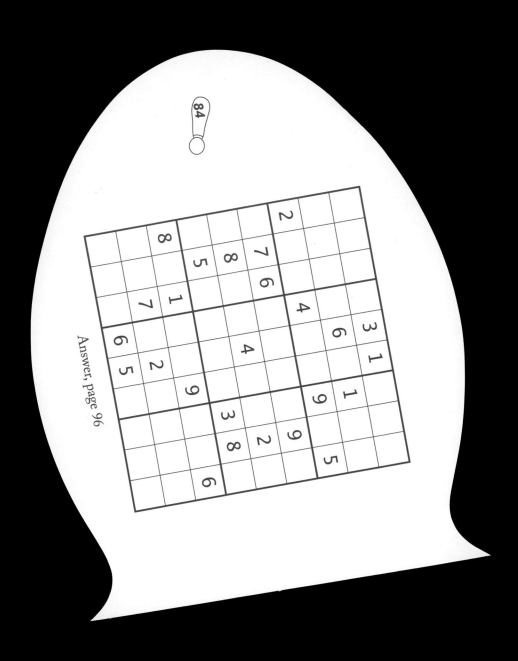

Answer, page 96

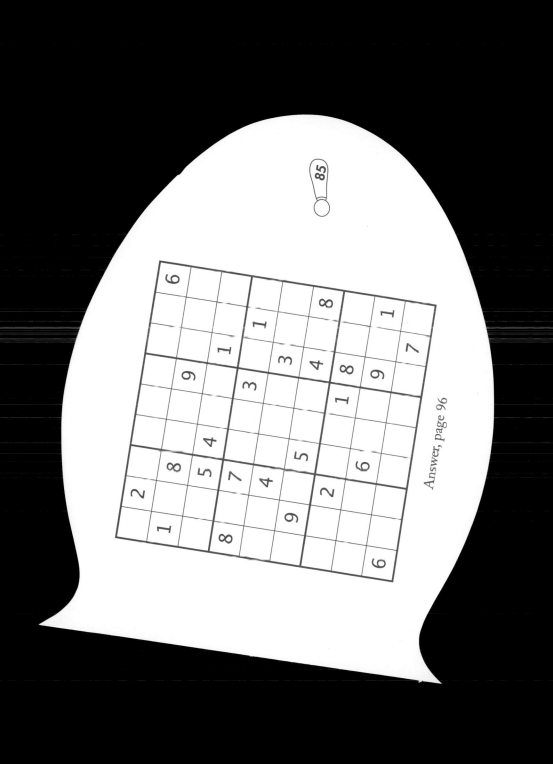

Answer, page 96

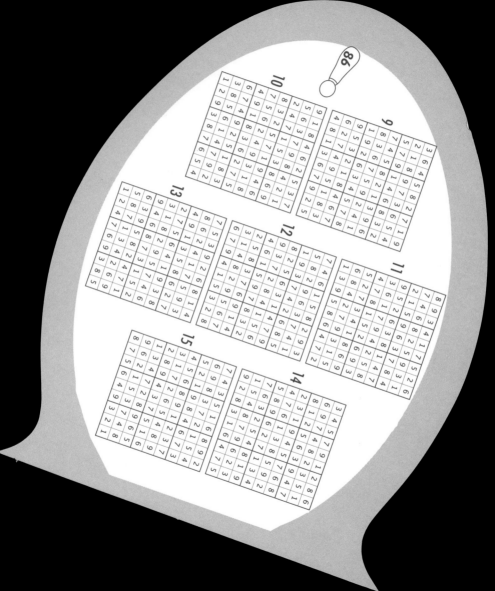

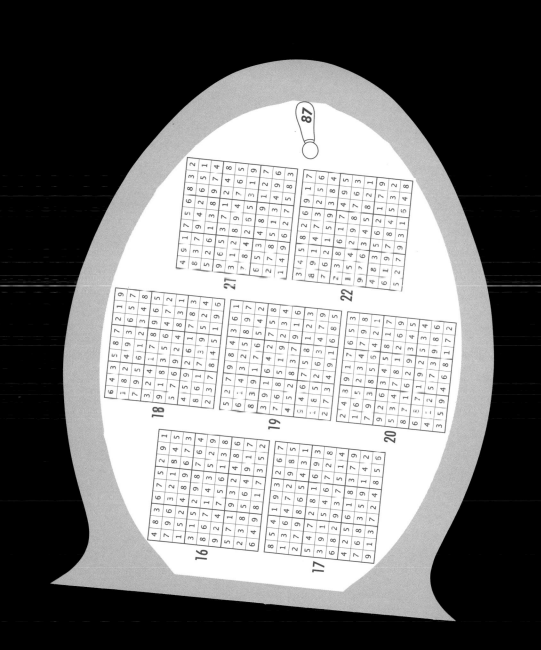

23

1	2	5	4	3	6	9	8	7
7	4	8	2	5	9	3	1	6
6	3	9	8	1	7	5	4	2
5	9	1	7	8	4	2	6	3
2	8	3	6	9	1	4	7	5
4	6	7	5	2	3	1	9	8
9	5	6	1	7	2	8	3	4
8	1	4	3	6	5	7	2	9
3	7	2	9	4	8	6	5	1

24

5	2	7	8	6	4	9	1	3
3	9	6	7	2	1	4	5	8
1	8	4	9	5	3	6	2	7
4	1	9	2	7	8	5	3	6
2	6	5	3	1	9	8	7	4
7	3	8	6	4	5	2	9	1
9	4	3	1	8	2	7	6	5
8	7	2	5	3	6	1	4	9
6	5	1	4	9	7	3	8	2

25

3	9	8	5	7	6	1	4	2
1	6	2	9	4	8	5	7	3
5	4	7	1	3	2	8	9	6
2	5	4	7	6	1	9	3	8
6	7	9	3	8	5	4	2	1
8	1	3	4	2	9	6	5	7
9	3	6	2	1	4	7	8	5
7	8	5	6	9	3	2	1	4
4	2	1	8	5	7	3	6	9

26

3	4	2	8	9	1	7	5	6
9	1	7	5	3	6	2	4	8
6	5	8	4	7	2	1	9	3
5	2	6	3	1	4	9	8	7
1	8	3	9	5	7	6	2	4
4	7	9	2	6	8	5	3	1
2	9	1	7	4	3	8	6	5
7	3	5	6	8	9	4	1	2
8	6	4	1	2	5	3	7	9

27

8	1	2	7	3	6	9	5	4
9	6	3	5	8	4	1	7	2
5	4	7	1	9	2	3	6	8
7	5	8	9	6	1	2	4	3
2	9	6	3	4	8	5	1	7
4	3	1	2	5	7	8	9	6
6	2	4	8	1	5	7	3	9
3	8	5	6	7	9	4	2	1
1	7	9	4	2	3	6	8	5

28

9	1	5	2	4	7	6	8	3
4	7	8	9	6	3	5	2	1
6	3	2	8	5	1	7	9	4
8	6	4	3	9	5	2	1	7
7	2	1	4	8	6	9	3	5
5	9	3	1	7	2	4	6	8
3	5	6	7	2	8	1	4	9
1	4	7	6	3	9	8	5	2
2	8	9	5	1	4	3	7	6

29

4	1	8	5	3	7	6	2	9
2	7	6	9	8	1	4	3	5
5	3	9	6	4	2	1	7	8
6	4	1	8	7	3	5	9	2
8	2	5	4	9	6	7	1	3
3	9	7	2	1	5	8	6	4
7	5	3	1	2	4	9	8	6
9	6	2	7	5	8	3	4	1
1	8	4	3	6	9	2	5	7

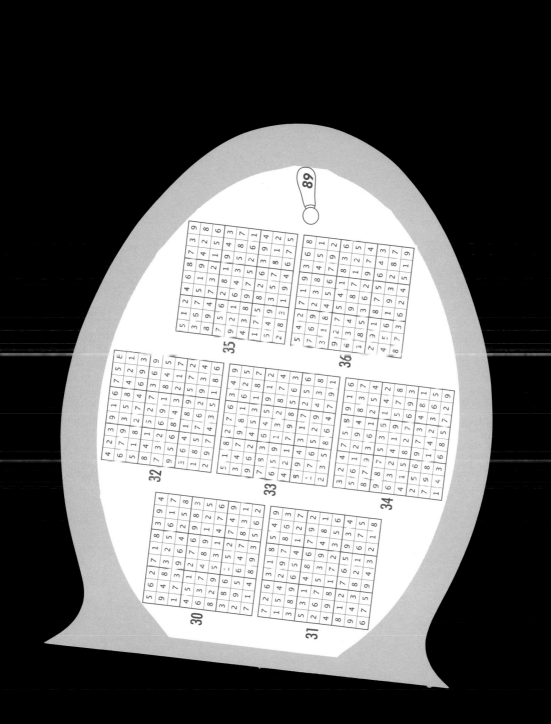

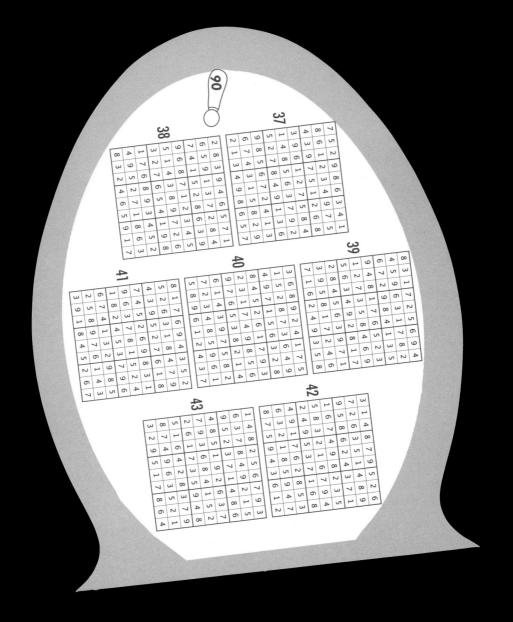

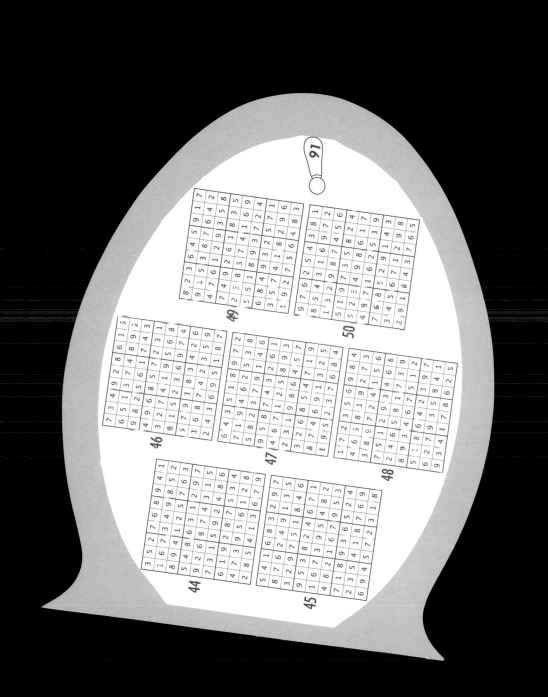

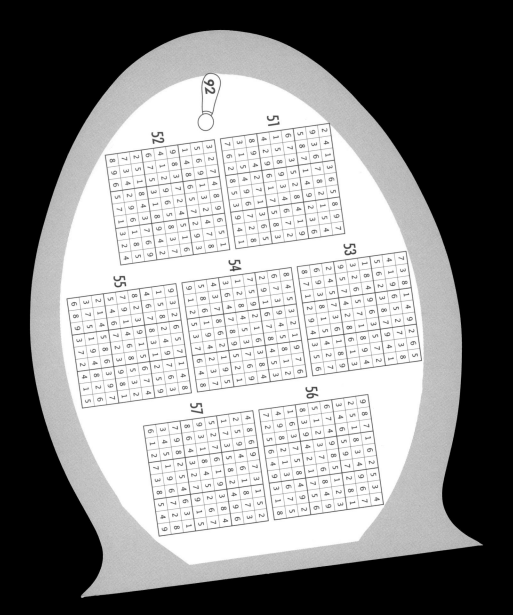

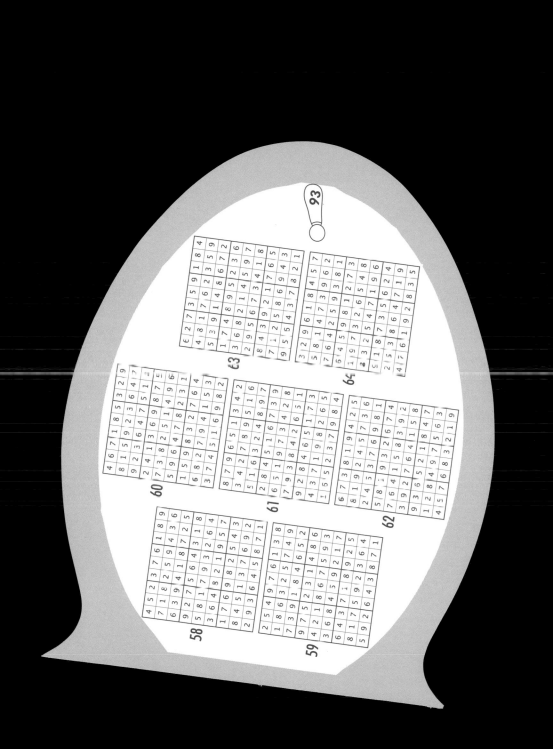

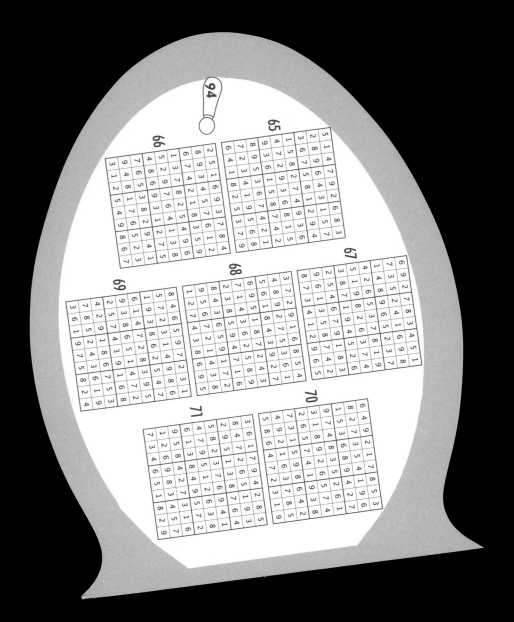

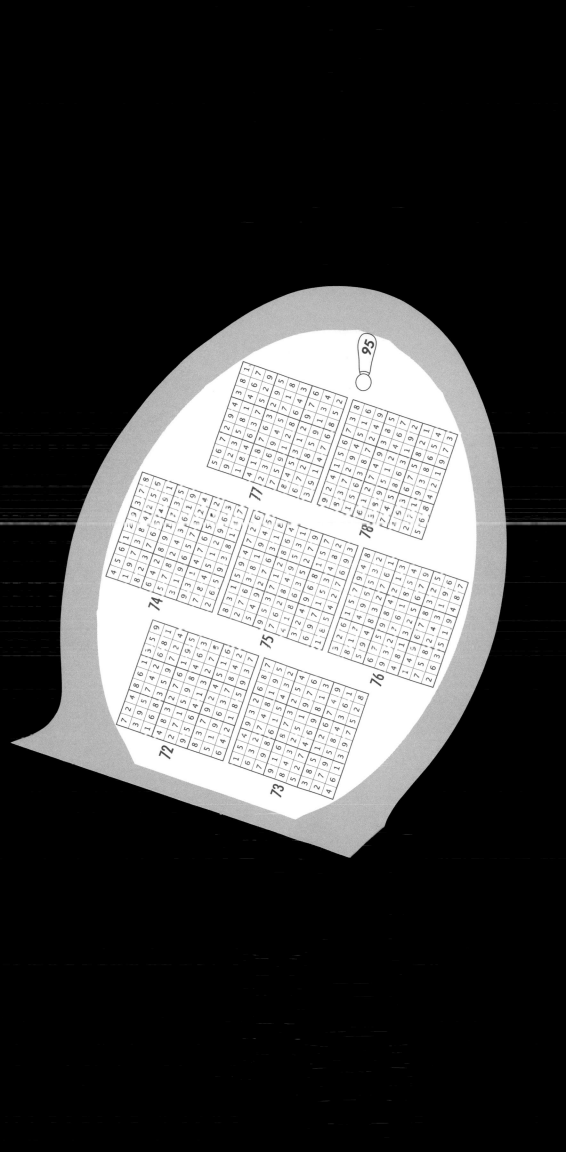

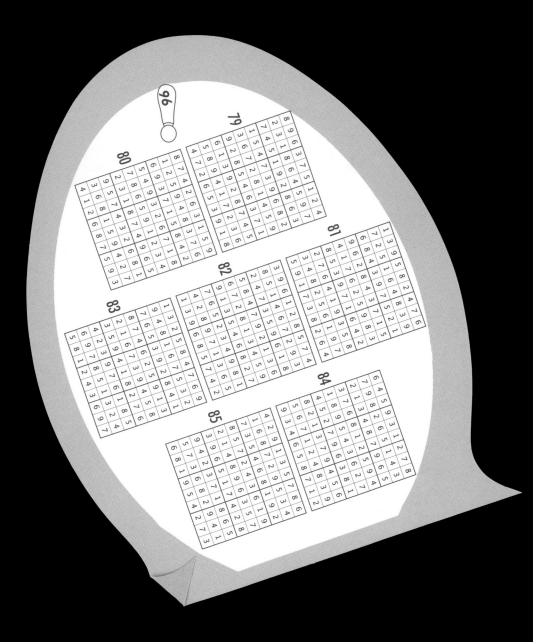